The Wonder of Early Years Teaching

The Wonder of Early Years Teaching

A Practical Guide to Nurturing Young Minds

Rebecca Underwood

1 Oliver's Yard
55 City Road
London EC1Y 1SP

2455 Teller Road
Thousand Oaks
California 91320

10th Floor, Emaar Capital Tower 2
MG Road, Sikanderpur, Sector 26
Gurugram, Haryana – 122002
India

8 Marina View Suite 43-053
Asia Square Tower 1
Singapore 018960

Editor: Amy Thornton
Editorial assistant: Harry Dixon
Production editor: Sarah Sewell
Copyeditor: Martin Noble
Proofreader: Thea Watson
Marketing manager: Lucy Sofroniou
Cover design: Wendy Scott
Typeset by: C&M Digitals (P) Ltd, Chennai, India

© Rebecca Underwood 2026

Apart from any fair dealing for the purposes of research, private study, or criticism or review, as permitted under the Copyright, Designs and Patents Act, 1988, this publication may not be reproduced, stored or transmitted in any form, or by any means, without the prior permission in writing of the publisher, or in the case of reprographic reproduction, in accordance with the terms of licences issued by the Copyright Licensing Agency. Enquiries concerning reproduction outside those terms should be sent to the publisher.

Library of Congress Control Number: 2025937476

British Library Cataloguing in Publication data

A catalogue record for this book is available from the British Library

ISBN 978-1-0362-0857-8
ISBN 978-1-0362-0856-1 (pbk)

Contents

About the Author and This Book   vii
Acknowledgements   ix

1   Setting the Stage for Wonder   1

2   Cast and Crew: Building and Maintaining Strong Relationships   5

3   Lights, Camera, Action: Crafting a Magical Environment   23

4   Sound Check: Unlocking Language Development   45

5   Playtime Symphony: Where Learning Comes Alive   61

6   Directing the Journey: Planning, Performing and Reflecting   73
       6.1 The EYFS Framework   75
       6.2 The Areas of Learning and Development   87
       6.3 Planning Your Pedagogy   103

7   Final Curtain Call: Inspiring Early Years Educators Everywhere   113

Index   117

About the Author and This Book

As a teacher and lifelong advocate for the Early Years, I have spent over two decades working in classrooms where young children begin to make sense of the world; through story, through play, through careful teaching that honours who they are and who they are becoming. These are the years that shape everything that follows. My work has always returned to this beginning: the simplicity, the depth and the quiet power of getting it right from the very start.

The Wonder of Early Years Teaching was born from those years of watching, listening and learning. It is a guide, not to lead or instruct, but to walk beside you through the ever-changing, deeply human work of teaching young children. It was written for teachers who care deeply, who notice the small things and who strongly believe that joy and rigour belong side by side.

Over the years, I've worn many hats – class teacher, phase leader, deputy head, co-headteacher, Initial Teacher Training (ITT) Course Lead, school improvement advisor and now an education researcher. I've designed professional learning for trusts, supported early career teachers across the country and now proudly work with the National Institute of Teaching, helping to connect educational research with real practice, grounded in the needs of children and the professionals who teach them. Though my work now spans research and sector-wide support, my heart remains at the edge of the carpet – picture book in hand, sharing stories with children full of questions and wide-eyed wonder.

Looking back, I don't remember timetables or targets, but the laughter that danced through the room and the gentle shift when learning truly landed – that's what made it extraordinary. Teaching in Reception will always hold the highlight reel of my career: the transformation, the trust, the joy. The wonderful experiences I've gathered along the way, the children I've taught, the colleagues I've walked beside and the lessons learned in both calm and storm, continue to shape who I am and how I work.

The Wonder of Early Years Teaching is a reflection of this path; a resource crafted to support, inspire and stand beside educators as they navigate the joys and challenges of Early Years education. It's my hope that this book serves as a trusted companion, offering both practical guidance and heartfelt encouragement to those dedicated to nurturing young minds.

Acknowledgements

To my dad (my hero) – thank you for listening, patiently and endlessly, as I shared every story, every wobble and every wonder from the classroom. You've heard it all – the laughter, the late-night worries, the moments that stayed with me long after the school bell – and you were always the first to say, 'You should write this down.' This book exists because you believed I should.

And to my late uncle – a drama teacher with a spirit too bold for the ordinary. Your joy for storytelling, your fearless imagination and your unwavering belief that learning should be lived and felt, continue to shape everything I do. You used to say, *'Let there be joy, fun, dance, banging of drums and colour … so much colour. Don't give them grey.'* Your words have lived in my classroom, echoed through this book and stayed with me far beyond the page. This is for you – full of colour … never grey.

1
Setting the Stage for Wonder

Our Foundational 'Why'

At the heart of every laughter-filled classroom, behind every meticulously planned activity and within the bright eyes of our youngest learners, lies our foundational 'why'; the profound belief in the transformative power of Early Years education. These critical years are the grand stage where young minds awaken, confidence takes root and a love of learning ignites. In this ever-evolving performance, children step into the spotlight as curious and resilient learners, ready to embrace the world with open hearts, eager minds and the courage to take centre stage in their own stories.

It is within these formative years that we, as passionate educators, have the unique opportunity to instil this passion for learning, weaving social and emotional growth into each precious moment, while supporting families in creating a strong foundation that prepares all children to navigate an ever-changing world. We stand united in our belief that getting it right in the Early Years is essential, not just as an investment in individual futures but in the future of our global community. Through dedication, creativity and unwavering support, we attempt to overcome the constant challenges presented by our precarious sector, ensuring that every single child is equipped with the tools and dispositions they need to thrive. Our joint mission extends beyond the classroom; we are builders of bridges between families and society, torchbearers of hope and change for Early Years education, and fierce advocates for every child's right to the best possible start in life. Early Years educators do so much more than teach; they nurture, inspire and transform lives, and I have yet to meet one who does not carry that passion in their heart.

Children thrive when their needs are met across all domains, including emotional, social, language and physical needs, as well as throughout their own personal learning journeys. Julian Grenier, EYFS expert, says:

> the early years are the crucial time for developing children's enjoyment of learning, their engagement and motivation. It's an important time for children to develop their ability to persist and show gritty determination.
>
> (Grenier 2020)

Devoted Early Years educators, like you, cherish the opportunity to nurture not only intellectual growth but emotional and social development, laying a solid foundation for lifelong learning and well-being for all children. This creates an educational experience that is as enriching for us as it is for the children, woven with moments of wonder, connection, and the joy of learning side by side.

> All children deserve the care and support they need to have the best start in life. Children learn and develop at a faster rate from birth to five years old than at any other time in their lives, so their experiences in early years have a major impact on their future life chances
>
> (Department for Education 2025)

The Nature of Our Role

Yet, as we navigate the challenging but rewarding world of Early Years education, there's a pressing need for society to recognise the intense nature of our daily practice. The landscape of early education has undergone significant transformations since my initiation into the field in 1996, when I commenced my BA Hons with QTS at the University of the West of England, Bristol. Although recently, there have been notable advancements for the better, there are still many barriers and frustrations in Early Years education that we face as a sector. SEND (Special Educational Needs and Disabilities) referrals are on the rise, mirroring the growing complexity of need within classrooms, while staffing levels dwindle alarmingly, stretching resources terribly thin. This harsh reality brings to light the critical need for a heightened focus and new-found respect placed on Early Years education, not just as a fundamental phase of learning but as a pivotal point where early intervention can shape life trajectories.

As educators, we adapt, innovate and pour our hearts into our vocation, so the time has come for a collective recognition of the indispensable role Early Years plays in building a resilient, inclusive society and for it to receive the investment and recognition it has long deserved. Let me be clear: it is not my intention to lament over the many trials we face in Early Years education: instead, this is a clarion call to celebrate the unmatched glories of EYFS, to entice fresh talent into our ranks and to rejuvenate those disheartened (quite rightly) by the rise in systemic hurdles. I do believe change is not just on the horizon but already underway. The direction was set in motion by the 2021 EYFS reforms and carried forward in the latest statutory framework (Department for Education 2025), the evolving standards set by Ofsted and the publishing of research projects conducted by the Department for Education in the *Best Start in Life: A Research Review for Early Years* (Department for Education 2024a) and the EEF's (Education Endowment Foundation) *Early Years Evidence Store* (EEF 2022). While we may still face many challenges, it's essential to recognise and embrace the positive shifts that have occurred in recent years. Alone, our impact may resemble solitary actors on an empty stage but together, we possess the power to orchestrate a chorus of transformation that resonates throughout the entire theatre of education.

The 'Theatre' of the Early Years

Embedded within the pages of my book, you'll notice a recurring motif of 'theatre': this is not only a deliberate and playful nod to my deep-seated love for the creative arts but also a tribute to a profoundly influential figure in my life: my late uncle. He wasn't just a relative but a guiding light in my journey into teaching, embodying what I believe to be the epitome of a 'teacher' – a drama teacher no less. His vibrant spirit along with his own inspirational mantra have echoed throughout my EYFS mind and glorious career. His words, 'Let there be joy, fun, dance, banging of drums and colour ... so much colour. Don't give them grey', have not only shaped my teaching and leadership philosophies but have also become a beacon that illuminates the essence of this book and my outlook on education. I can only imagine his heartbreak at the narrowing of education, the dimming of creativity and the quieting of joyful noise in so many classrooms today. It is my mission to keep that spirit alive; to champion curiosity and ensure that every child experiences the richness of learning, full of awe, wonder and endless discovery.

So, picture the scene: A bustling classroom filled with the excited chatter of young learners, each eager to embark on a new day of exploration and discovery. The provision ready, brimming with possibilities and endless learning opportunities. As you glance around, you're greeted by the smiling faces of your dedicated colleagues, all keen to build on the successes of yesterday and make today even more memorable. The parents offering a supportive smile or a reassuring word as they drop off their little ones. Their involvement and partnership adding a layer of warmth and encouragement to the vibrant atmosphere. All is in place, hearts are full, and the day ahead awaits. If you read this and get goosebumps, then this is the book for you, and you and I will get on like a 'Wendy' house on fire! This is honestly what I felt for the majority of my career; happiness, contentment, a profound sense of purpose and belonging, feeling valued and making a difference at every opportunity. It was a time when I truly felt like a professional, empowered to inspire and shape the futures of the young minds entrusted to my care.

Within these pages, I endeavour to highlight the unparalleled joy that permeates Early Years education. It's about those magical moments, the 'wow' experiences that ignite curiosity and spark lifelong learning. At its core, it's *always* about the children; their boundless potential, their unique journeys and the profound impact we have as their privileged educators. In essence, this book serves as a poignant reminder of the deep and lasting influence of Early Years education and the imperative to 'get it right' within these crucial Early Years. I seek to highlight the importance of laying sturdy foundations for children, for when we nurture their earliest years, we unlock the doors to a future radiant with boundless dreams.

Furthermore, I'll provide a treasure trove of ideas and practical tips for you to incorporate creativity into your daily lessons. Whether through open-ended art activities, sensory play experiences or outdoor exploration, I'll showcase how play-based learning can be seamlessly integrated into the curriculum to engage children's interests and spark their imaginations. Join me as we embark on a playful journey filled with laughter, discovery and endless possibilities.

So, places everyone, quiet backstage.... and let the show begin!

References

Department for Education (DfE) (2024a) *Best Start in Life: A Research Review for Early Years.* Available at: www.gov.uk/government/publications/best-start-in-life-a-research-review-for-early-years

Department for Education (DfE) (2024b) *Early Years Foundation Stage Statutory Framework for Group and School-Based Providers.* Available at: https://assets.publishing.service.gov.uk/media/65aa5e42ed27ca001327b2c7/EYFS_statutory_framework_for_group_and_school_based_providers.pdf

Department for Education (DfE) (2025) *Early Years Foundation Stage Statutory Framework: For Group and School-Based Providers.* (effective 1 September 2025). London: Department for Education.

Education Endowment Foundation (EEF) (2022) Early Years Evidence Store. Available at: https://educationendowmentfoundation.org.uk/early-years/evidence-store

Grenier (2020) *Working with the Revised Early Years Foundation Stage: Principles into Practice.* Independently published: London. Available at: www.associatednurseries.co.uk/an/Working-with-the-revised-Early-Years-Foundation-Stage-Principles-reduced%20acr5.pdf

2
Cast and Crew

Building and Maintaining Strong Relationships

In the complex symphony of Early Years education, the harmonious collaboration of teachers, teaching assistants, wider school staff and parents forms the backdrop against which children take centre stage. In this chapter, we delve into the symbiotic connection between nurturing these essential relationships and how doing so cultivates a positive and successful classroom culture. We will discuss how each stakeholder truly enriches the educational experience for all others within your setting and how positive relationships are paramount when creating an environment conducive to growth and development for all; in particular, the children that we teach.

Classroom culture is the bedrock upon which the entire educational experience is built. It encompasses the values, expectations and practices that shape the entire learning environment and influence how children interact with one another and with their teachers. A positive classroom culture fosters a sense of belonging, encourages active engagement and promotes mutual respect. It is a dynamic entity, continuously evolving with the contributions of every individual within the school community. All stakeholders must play their parts, each contributing to the culture that brings the 'performance' to life.

As we explore strategies for building strong relationships across an Early Years setting, we will uncover how these interpersonal bonds serve as the foundation upon which a positive classroom culture can be built.

Building a Harmonious Team

Before delving into child and parent relationships, I believe that it is crucial to first focus on the relationships among staff members. A harmonious and supportive team of educators (and by educators, I refer to all classroom-based staff) sets the tone for the entire provision. When staff relationships are strong, a positive ripple effect occurs which permeates the entire learning environment… and beyond. Educators who feel valued and respected are more likely to collaborate effectively, share ideas and support one another innately, in turn creating a cohesive and nurturing environment that truly benefits the children. Mutual respect and teamwork are essential for building a truly supportive Early Years community of influential educators who are determined to make a real difference.

In recent years, evidence gathered from social media, research articles and the infamous 'educational grapevine' shows that the most common challenges facing Early Years settings remain unchanged: low morale, fractured school culture, inadequate pay, ineffective leadership and excessive workloads. Sound familiar? Retention also continues to be a persistent challenge, no doubt arising from these very factors, therefore, ensuring that staff feel valued and supported is vital, as high turnover unsettles children and leaves teams disjointed. Prioritising staff well-being, embedding strong support systems and providing ongoing and relevant professional development are all essential components for cultivating a committed and effective Early Years team. When we invest in the strength and stability of our team, we create a consistent and nurturing environment that is fundamental to the growth and development of the children in our care. Ultimately, it is the collaboration and authenticity among staff and the culture this cultivates that form the foundations of a thriving setting.

I've been incredibly fortunate to work with such dedicated and caring teaching assistants and fellow teachers over the years who have made each day not only easier but also profoundly more enjoyable. This wasn't by accident; it was the result of intentional and authentic leadership and a shared commitment to excellence. As the class teacher, I took the lead in cultivating this environment, recognising that leadership isn't confined to titles or positions. Whether you hold the title of EYFS lead or class teacher, you are a leader in your own right with the capacity to drive consistency and build strong relationships at every interval. Your every action and daily attitude set the tone, guiding others and ensuring that a unified, supportive environment is maintained for everyone involved.

One teaching assistant I was lucky enough to work alongside was exceptional in every sense. She consistently brought her strengths and initiatives to the table, always anticipating what was needed while using every second of her precious time to enhance the children's daily experiences. Above all, she genuinely cared. Our bond was strong because we worked on it daily, ensuring we were each other's eyes and ears and always child focused. We communicated effortlessly, often referring to our vision or key objective for each session, acknowledging aspects of the Early Years Framework and highlighting children's passions and moments of development at every opportunity. This deep connection and mutual understanding didn't develop overnight; it was nurtured through dedication, graft, reciprocal respect and a shared commitment to children's happiness and well-being.

I must acknowledge here that a teaching assistant's day may start later and finish earlier than a teacher's and it's crucial that we respect this. They have every right to leave at 3pm, so instead of extending their time, it's critical to create intervals throughout the day to connect, review and plan forward. Yes, time is always scarce in an Early Years classroom but by embedding effective routines and consistent assessment procedures so deeply into your practice, you can find ways to maximise every precious moment. In my experience, over time, our working relationship became so finely tuned that we could convey our thoughts with just a raised eyebrow or a subtle point of the finger.

This level of collaboration, trust and respect was not just beneficial for us as professionals but was also palpably felt by the children. When the adults in the room are in sync and have the children's best interests at heart, an environment is created where every child can blossom. It's a powerful reminder that strong, supportive relationships among staff really are the foundation of a successful Early Years classroom. So how do we begin to create and sustain this firm foundation?

Defining and Expressing a Shared Vision

The first essential component is sharing your team vision or intent; this is crucial and everyone must be a part of this direction-setting process. You or your Early Years lead will start by clearly communicating the overall goals and values of your Early Years setting. This might be at the beginning of the year or part of a thorough induction process as new staff arrive. Pedagogy and curriculum will be key drivers here, with every aspect of your vision rooted in the child, shaped by your current cohort and also the community you serve.

An Early Years vision is a clear and inspiring statement that outlines your goals, values and aspirations. It serves as a guiding framework that shapes the overall approach to education and care within your Early Years setting. It is the golden thread that runs through every interaction, every decision, and every moment of play. A comprehensive vision reflects the core beliefs about how young children should be nurtured, educated and supported during their formative years.

Practical Tips 2.1

Aligning Your Team with Shared Goals

1 **Understand and connect with the vision:** A vision cannot inspire if it is not fully understood. Take time to immerse yourself in what it means, how it influences your daily practice and why it matters. Ask questions (no question is too silly), seek clarity, and reflect on how it aligns with your own values and approach to Early Years education. When you truly connect with your vision, it becomes a driving force behind your work.

2 **Shape it with your voice:** A powerful vision is not dictated from above; it is co-constructed. Share your insights, offer suggestions and engage in discussions

(Continued)

that help refine and enhance the vision. Every member of the team brings a unique perspective, and a vision that is shaped together carries more meaning and impact. Speak up, contribute and be part of the process.

3. **Live and breathe it every day:** A vision does not only belong in a handbook or pinned on a noticeboard; it belongs in the moments, the interactions and the everyday rhythm of your classroom. Carry it with you in the way you welcome a child, in the way you set up a learning space, in the way you encourage a hesitant learner to take a risk. A strong vision is felt, seen and heard in everything you do. Recognise that the vision is a collective mission. When everyone is aligned and working together from the same Early Years hymn sheet, it strengthens the team's sense of unity and purpose. Support one another in keeping it alive and highlight moments where it truly shines.

4. **Be open to change:** As the year progresses, expect the vision to evolve based on new challenges, opportunities or team changes. Be flexible and adaptable. Stay involved in discussions regarding changes and adjustments and ask questions if something isn't clear or if you need more information. When changes do occur, anchoring your perspective in the children's best interests can make new approaches feel more meaningful and worthwhile.

5. **Consider the bigger picture:** A vision is more than words on a page. It is a reflection of the children, the team and the community it serves. When supporting the vision, step back and see the whole landscape. Think about the children in your care, their needs, their stories and the rich tapestry of the community around them. What does this vision mean for them? How does it shape their daily experiences? A strong, purposeful vision is not a rigid blueprint; it is a living, breathing guide that flexes and grows in response to the children, the setting and the world beyond. Keep this in mind as you contribute, ensuring that every action, every choice and every moment of practice aligns with the intent – to create an environment where all children flourish, where learning is joyful and where the values at the heart of your setting are felt in every interaction.

Intrinsically linked to your vision is the need to fully understand and adhere to the statutory requirements. Every staff member must be fully aware of what is expected in this regard. These requirements are not just bureaucratic necessities; they are the bedrock of quality care and highly effective Early Years education. Ensuring that everyone maintains these standards is essential for the safety, well-being and development of the children in your care. The Early Years Framework document is your 'educational bible' here. Have multiple copies placed around the setting. Talk about this document daily; chant it, sing it, live it and breathe it.

Practical Tips 2.2

Staying Updated, Accountable and Engaged Through Proactive Practice

1. **Stay updated on safeguarding and policy updates:** Regularly review safeguarding procedures, ensuring they are embedded in your daily practice. If anything is unclear, ask questions, as there is no room for uncertainty when it comes to keeping children safe. Stay informed about key areas such as curriculum expectations and safeguarding protocols. Engage in regular discussions or briefings to refresh knowledge and maintain consistency across the team. Keep up to date with DfE updates, Ofsted reforms and sector-wide changes to ensure your practice remains current, compliant and reflective of best practice. Being well-informed not only strengthens your setting but also reinforces your confidence as an educator.

2. **Actively contribute to briefings:** Team meetings are vital opportunities to align, reflect and strengthen team practice. Come prepared to contribute, whether by sharing insights from recent training, discussing the needs of a key child or raising important observations that could support the team's collective growth. Use this time to ask questions, seek clarity and ensure everyone is on the same page. Active participation fosters a culture of collaboration, where every voice matters and every contribution helps shape a stronger, more responsive setting.

3. **Stay informed on daily responsibilities:** Use a shared notice board to track upcoming deadlines and activities, ensuring everyone knows their role in each task. Regular check-ins can clarify who is involved and help keep everyone aligned. Celebrate successes as a team to foster a positive and collaborative environment.

4. **Commit to ongoing professional development:** Engage in regular professional development opportunities to refine your skills, stay informed and support your team. This could be attending a training session, reading an article or listening to a podcast. Professional development doesn't have to feel overwhelming or consume large chunks of time – small, consistent efforts can make a big impact. A five-minute read, a quick discussion with a colleague or reflecting on a recent challenge can all contribute to your growth. The key is to stay curious, seek out learning in everyday moments and embrace development as a continuous journey rather than a daunting task.

5. **Foster a culture of trust:** Trust is the foundation of a thriving Early Years setting, built through consistency, integrity and a commitment to best practice. By adhering to statutory requirements, safeguarding procedures and high-quality provision, you reassure parents, children and the wider community that their well-being is at the heart of everything you do. Trust grows through transparency, reliability and creating a setting where families feel confident, children feel secure and staff feel valued.

For your vision to truly resonate, it is also imperative that staff possess a deep and nuanced understanding of child development. They must not only observe children's interests but also delve into the underlying reasons and motivations that drive these behaviours and ideas. Staff are the navigators of each child's journey, guiding them with care, ensuring that they move in the right direction and at a pace that honours their individual developmental needs. Regularly engage in discussions that explore the characteristics of effective teaching and learning, as outlined in the Early Years Foundation Stage Framework. Focus on key teaching strategies that have proven successful in your setting, ensuring they align with the principles of playing and exploring, active learning and creating and thinking critically. By continuously reflecting on and refining these approaches, you can enhance the learning environment and support the development of every child.

Child development is akin to a theatre production, where each child's unique journey unfolds unpredictably, with moments of rapid progress and periods of reflection, defying any rigid script or checklist. To fully support this journey, it is essential for educators to engage in regular, meaningful discussions about the children. This ongoing communication allows staff to connect insights and observations, creating a comprehensive understanding of each child's development. By linking these conversations to the 'bigger picture', educators can more effectively support and guide each child's individual path.

Moreover, staff must be acutely aware of the concept of cultural capital; the rich tapestry of knowledge, skills and experiences that children bring from their diverse backgrounds. This understanding is crucial for creating meaningful connections between a child's home life and their educational experiences, allowing staff to build bridges that support and enhance learning. It is particularly important to ensure that disadvantaged children receive the best possible education, as these connections can play a vital role in closing gaps, fostering equity and providing all children with the opportunities they need to succeed.

An awareness of the Matthew Effect is important here, which underscores the profound impact of early educational experiences. Those who start with an advantage often see that advantage grow, while those children who begin with less support or opportunity may continue to face widening gaps. Staff must be vigilant in recognising these dynamics and must be committed to providing *all* children with the opportunities they need to thrive. By weaving these profound insights into their practice, staff can help cultivate an environment where high expectations and belief in each child's ability to succeed are central – regardless of their starting point.

Effective Communication

Effective communication is fundamental in any Early Years setting. When team members are involved in the decision-making process, they gain a sense of ownership and accomplishment, strengthening the foundations of a more cohesive work environment. When communication is transparent, and the focus is on collaboratively finding solutions that best benefit the children and staff team, it encourages everyone to engage;

collective ownership is essential here. Communicate with kindness and clarity – listen with intent, respond with empathy and let your words reflect the values of your setting. In environments where collaboration and learning are continuous, the way feedback is given can uplift, inspire and drive positive change. When delivered with care and purpose, feedback becomes a tool for progress rather than a source of doubt, creating a community where everyone, children and educators alike, feels valued, motivated and empowered to move forward.

Child-centred, meaningful discussions are crucial to children's development and all staff play a vital role in this process. By collectively sharing insights and observations, we can tailor teaching methods and materials to meet the diverse needs of individual learners. This might involve varying the levels of support provided, offering multiple ways for children to engage with content or allowing for different methods of demonstrating understanding. For example, while some children may benefit from visual aids, others might thrive with hands-on activities or verbal explanations. When everyone contributes their perspectives, we build a more comprehensive and effective approach, ensuring that each child's unique learning style is respected and supported.

Regular check-ins, like morning briefings or end-of-day reflections, are priceless opportunities to share observations, address concerns and celebrate successes. These candid discussions help ensure everyone is aligned and responsive to the children's evolving needs.

Enthusiasm, positivity and vigour are also essential qualities that can energise a learning environment and inspire both children and staff. When educators bring a lively spirit and a positive attitude to their work, it creates an atmosphere which drives curiosity and where challenges are met with greater optimism. Enthusiasm is contagious; it motivates others to engage fully, take initiative and approach their tasks with a sense of real purpose. By embodying these qualities, you not only enhance the overall mood and productivity of the team but also offer children a living lesson in how to meet challenge with courage.

Practical Tips 2.3

Building Trust and Collaboration to Foster Team Unity

1. **Be present:** Engage fully in team discussions, whether in meetings or casual conversations. Your voice matters. Being present isn't just about showing up; it's about actively listening, contributing ideas and valuing the perspectives of those around you. No question is too trivial. Stay tuned in during morning briefings or end-of-day reflections, as these moments offer valuable opportunities to align

(Continued)

with your colleagues, celebrate successes and navigate challenges together. If decisions are made that impact your work or the children, don't hesitate to ask for the reasons behind them. Understanding the 'why' helps you stay aligned with the team's goals.

2. **Share your observations:** Regularly share insights about the children you work with. Discussing their needs and progress with your team helps tailor the learning experience and ensures every child gets the support they need. Make sure your conversations with colleagues always focus on what's best for the children. Whether you're planning an activity or discussing classroom challenges, keeping the children at the heart of your discussions ensures a shared sense of purpose.

3. **Use respectful communication:** Listen actively, show empathy and give constructive feedback. Positive communication builds trust and strengthens relationships within the team. By giving your full attention, acknowledging everyone's perspectives and responding thoughtfully, you demonstrate genuine respect for their opinions and experiences.

4. **Show small acts of kindness:** Whether it's offering a helping hand, giving a word of encouragement or simply listening with empathy, small acts of kindness create a culture where everyone feels valued and respected.

5. **Support a culture of shared responsibility:** A strong team thrives on mutual support and accountability. Take ownership of your role while recognising that you are part of something bigger. Every contribution, no matter how small, helps create a positive learning environment. If challenges arise, approach them as a team, seeking solutions together rather than working in isolation. Offer help freely, seek support confidently, and trust that collaboration will always lead to stronger outcomes for both staff and children.

Reflective Practices

True improvement begins with honest reflection. Regularly taking the time to assess and evaluate your practices allows you to identify what's working well and where adjustments are needed. Reflective practice encourages continuous learning and growth, both for the individual and the team. By reflecting on key experiences and outcomes, you can make informed decisions that drive positive change and enhance the overall effectiveness of your approaches.

Action research is a powerful tool for continuous improvement in education. It involves educators systematically investigating their own practices to address specific challenges or questions within their setting. By engaging in action research, teachers can identify areas for improvement, implement changes and assess the impact of those changes in real time.

This cyclical process of planning, acting, observing and reflecting, allows educators to make informed decisions that are directly relevant to their unique context. Whether it's experimenting with new teaching strategies, refining classroom management techniques or enhancing children's engagement, action research empowers educators to be proactive and reflective. It bridges the gap between theory and practice, ensuring that changes are evidence-based and tailored to the needs of the children and the learning environment.

Practical Tips 2.4

Ongoing Growth and Improvement for Reflective Educators

1. **Read up on new research and ideas:** Stay up to date with Early Years educational research and reflect on how new theories or strategies can improve your practice. Constant learning keeps your teaching fresh and effective.
2. **Ask for feedback from peers, parents and the children:** Gain a well-rounded perspective by asking for feedback from colleagues, parents and, where possible, the children. Each group can provide unique insights through brief conversations, surveys or feedback forms, often highlighting areas for development that you may not have noticed.
3. **Use reflection journals:** Encourage staff to keep an informal reflection journal where they can jot down thoughts, challenges, successes and areas for improvement. Writing things down helps clarify thinking and can be a useful reference for future discussions. Alternatively, have an EYFS journal or communication book for the whole team to add to. Always link your reflections back to the children's experiences and outcomes. Consider how your actions, decisions and teaching strategies are impacting their learning and well-being and make amendments where necessary.
4. **Use video or audio recording:** Record lessons or activities (with appropriate permissions) and review them together later. Watching or listening to your interactions can provide valuable insights into your teaching practices and areas for improvement. Recording quality interactions with staff and children is incredibly powerful, allowing you to build a 'resource bank' of good practice. In one of my settings, we recorded staff engaging in these activities, and the videos were shared with other schools as exemplary materials, highlighting our high standards and effective methods.
5. **Focus on one area at a time:** Choose a specific aspect of your teaching to reflect on – whether it's behaviour management, adaptive teaching, questioning techniques, scaffolding learning, enhancing continuous provision or supporting children's language development. Focusing on one area at a time allows you to dig deeper, refine your approach and make achievable, sustained improvements.

(Continued)

> Small, intentional changes lead to lasting impact, strengthening both your practice and the learning experiences you create for children.
>
> 6   **Experiment with new approaches:** Try out new teaching strategies and reflect on their impact. Use action research to assess what works in real time and adjust your approach accordingly. Changes don't have to be mammoth; small tweaks can have a big impact! You might introduce calming music as children enter the classroom to create a peaceful atmosphere, trial a rolling snack time to encourage independence and reduce transitions or embed drama activities to bring stories and learning to life. The key is to be open, reflective and responsive, daring to try, to tweak, to transform – knowing that even the smallest changes can set great things in motion.

The fundamental aim is to create a harmonious environment where every member of the team feels valued and supported, much like a well-rehearsed theatre ensemble. When staff are genuinely happy and their emotional well-being is nurtured, they are able to perform at their best, bringing the entire 'production' to life with energy, passion and excellence.

In summary, the importance of staff relationships in shaping classroom culture cannot be overstated. At the heart of every thriving classroom lies a network of genuine connections, where every single adult that works in the provision, irrespective of hierarchy, is united by a shared sense of purpose and mutual respect. By nurturing these connections and cultivating a sense of belonging for all, we lay the foundations for a supportive community where individuals feel valued, empowered and inspired to excel. And remember, positive relationships require consistent effort and attention to stay strong. It's like trying to keep a theatre ensemble energised and in sync for every performance; it's no small task but the repercussions are immense.

Parental Engagement and Involvement: Parents in the Wings Supporting the Educational Performance

Recognising the significant impact of collaboration between home and school, 'the benefits are greatest when practitioners and families work in respectful partnership to develop ways to support children both at home and in the setting' (Early Education 2021). With this in mind, we will now explore practical strategies to strengthen these vital connections, ensuring that parents feel welcome, well informed and genuinely valued as partners in their child's learning journey throughout this crucial year.

Parents are the steady thread that weaves home and school together, shaping the way a child learns, grows and thrives. Their involvement is vital. When strong relationships are built, engagement follows and, with it, a deeper understanding of their child's world.

Yet, this connection doesn't always come easily. It takes time, trust and open doors. But when parents feel valued, when they are welcomed as partners in their child's journey, something powerful happens. They are more likely to engage, to listen, to play an active role. With the right support, they can build confidence in their own ability to nurture learning at home. Include them, inform them and share successes, because when parents and educators stand side by side, the child stands taller.

Parents and families must be integral to your vision. They likely chose your classroom because they resonate with your vision and philosophies, making it essential to involve them in the ongoing process of celebration and adaptation. However, it's essential here to recognise and understand the many barriers that may hinder parental engagement. Common challenges may include time constraints, language barriers, financial concerns and a lack of confidence in how to support their child's learning at home. By being aware of these barriers, you can tailor your approach to better meet the needs of all families, making it easier for them to engage and contribute to their child's education.

I greatly admire these statements in the *Birth to 5 Matters* document:

- *Parents make a crucial difference to children's outcomes.*
- *Parents are children's first and most enduring educators.*
- *Each unique family must be welcomed and listened to.*
- *Consider levels of engagement to make the most of relating to parents.*
- *Practitioners have a responsibility to work with all families.*
- *Clear leadership regarding partnership with parents will provide the right foundation.* (Early Education 2021)

Long-term parental engagement is built on trust, respect and mutual understanding. When settings 'value parents and carers as children's first educators' and provide opportunities for them to 'contribute to the whole of their child's journey' (DfE 2021b), it nurtures a sense of shared responsibility, empowering families and educators to support children together. Encouraging regular feedback, adapting strategies to meet families' needs, keeping parents well informed and celebrating their child's successes all contribute to a prosperous Early Years community.

Community Engagement: The Extended Cast

The word 'community' extends far beyond the physical boundaries of a school or Early Years setting. It alludes to the network of relationships, shared values and mutual support that surrounds children and their families. 'Community' encompasses not only the parents and carers but also local businesses, cultural institutions, services and even the natural environment in which the setting operates.

For EYFS teachers, embracing community means recognising the rich, varied resources available and incorporating them into the children's educational experience. Schools must be proactive in building relationships with local organisations, businesses and cultural institutions. This might involve inviting guest speakers from the community, organising trips to local libraries, museums and parks, or collaborating with local artisans or business owners to enrich classroom projects. Such partnerships provide real-world learning opportunities that extend beyond the classroom and ground children's education in the world around them.

Involving the community also means taking a vested interest in its 'well-being'. EYFS teachers can promote events that celebrate local culture, encourage children and families to participate in community-driven initiatives, or collaborate with local charities and services to offer support. Incorporating community engagement into your Early Years curriculum not only enriches children's learning by providing diverse, real-world experiences but also reinforces the idea that 'it takes a village to raise a child' (Clinton 1996). This approach highlights community as a vital source of moral growth and social connection, supporting children's sense of belonging and shared responsibility within their broader environment.

Building Relationships with Children: The Heart of the Performance

When the foundation of strong relationships with staff and parents is in place, the ultimate beneficiaries are the children. Yet, the relationships you build directly with the children are the heart of this entire performance. Just as in a great theatre production where the connection between the actors and the audience is what brings the story to life, the connections you form with each child are what truly counts. When children feel genuinely seen, heard and valued by the adults around them, they step into their roles with confidence and enthusiasm, they embrace learning with open hearts, ready to explore, create, and light up the stage.

At the earliest opportunity, take the time to truly know each child's unique character; their strengths, their fears, their passions, their quirks, their idiosyncrasies ... the little ways that make them uniquely them. Engage with them authentically, listen to their stories and show them that their voices matter. This deep, genuine connection acts as the invisible thread that ties them to the learning environment, making them feel safe, valued and understood.

High-quality interactions with young children stand as one of the most powerful determinants of their future success, particularly for those from disadvantaged backgrounds. In reshaping the EYFS Framework in 2021, the DfE acknowledged a fundamental truth: relationships matter. It is within the warmth of daily interactions, the back-and-forth of conversation and the trust between educator and child that real progress happens. Learning is far too dynamic, too rich, too alive to be reduced to paperwork. Instead, educators must be trusted to know their children deeply, to nurture their voices and to speak with confidence about their progress and growth. Every daily interaction with a child is a 'mini scene' that contributes to the overarching narrative of their development story and in the eyes of a child, the smallest moments mean everything; connection is where true learning begins.

Peer to Peer Relationships: Building the Ensemble

Step into an EYFS classroom, and you'll see it: the unspoken language of childhood. The whispered negotiations of who gets the next turn, the comforting pat on the back when things don't go quite right or the subtle delegations of role-play roles. The way children connect, collaborate and communicate really does shape the energy in the room and the depth of their play. Children's relationships with each other are a vital component of a thriving classroom environment.

Contributing significantly to both the social-emotional development and the overall learning experiences of all learners, these dynamic connections help children develop crucial skills such as communication, cooperation, empathy and conflict resolution. To encourage these strong, supportive peer relationships, it's essential to create a classroom culture that values collaboration and mutual respect.

Behaviour, in its rawest form, is communication. Every push, every hug, every eye-roll, every shared glance; they are all ways of navigating the social world. Children need to feel safe before they can take social risks, before they can fully step into friendships. The way we shape the environment, be that the praise we give, the boundaries we hold, the warmth in our approach; guides them towards positive, respectful relationships. Celebrating acts of kindness and cooperation within the classroom further reinforces positive behaviours and cultivates a culture where every child feels valued and connected.

Children watch adults. They absorb how we speak to them, how we interact with others, how we resolve conflict. They become what they see. If respect is modelled, they will show it. If emotions are acknowledged, they will name them. If kindness is valued, they will carry it into their friendships. So, we must create space for talk, for play, for connection.

Rich circle time discussions, collaborative projects and shared problem-solving activities provide purposeful opportunities for children to interact, share ideas and work together and become team mates. Incorporating games that require teamwork can also strengthen bonds and teach the importance of listening, turn-taking and valuing diverse perspectives. We teach them that words have weight, that friendships take time, that it's okay to make mistakes but, ultimately, that making the right choices matters. We celebrate the small victories: the hand held out in apology, the quiet inclusion of someone on the edges, the child who finally finds their voice. Some step through the door already fluent in the art of conversation, turn-taking and negotiation. Others are just beginning to find their voice, learning how to share space, how to listen, how to belong. Many arrive with fewer social skills than before, impacted by changing family dynamics, screen time replacing face-to-face interaction or fewer opportunities to engage in unstructured play. How they interact with each other and form relationships is essential, shaping not only their own daily experiences but the rhythm and culture of the entire setting. And so, our role as educators is more crucial than ever.

The way children connect with one another shapes everything; the learning, the culture, the joy in the room. And when they get it right, when they build those relationships with care, the classroom doesn't just work, it shines.

Practical Tips 2.5
How to Support Peer-to-Peer Relationships

1. **Facilitate circle time for connection:** Use daily or weekly circle time to encourage children to share thoughts, feelings and ideas. Incorporate activities that prompt discussions about kindness, respect and teamwork, creating a safe space for children to connect and learn about each other. Share thought-provoking photographs that spark conversation about different key themes such as kindness, morality or emotions.
2. **Organise collaborative projects:** Plan group activities where children work together to achieve a shared goal, such as creating a large mural, building a big junk model or solving puzzles. These projects encourage communication, cooperation and appreciation of each other's strengths.
3. **Teach and model conflict resolution:** Introduce simple strategies for resolving disagreements, such as taking turns to speak, using 'I feel' statements and brainstorming solutions together. Model these behaviours during classroom interactions to reinforce their importance.
4. **Encourage mixed-age or buddy systems:** Pair younger children with older peers or create buddy systems for specific activities. These pairings help children build relationships, learn from each other and develop empathy and patience.
5. **Create inclusive play opportunities:** Set up play areas that encourage group interactions, such as a role-play shop, outdoor obstacle course or nature scavenger hunt. Ensure the materials and activities are accessible and inviting to all children, fostering inclusive and collaborative play.
6. **Celebrate and reinforce positive interactions:** Highlight acts of kindness, cooperation and teamwork during the day. Use a kindness board, stickers or verbal praise to acknowledge and celebrate these moments, reinforcing a culture of respect and collaboration. The 'Treasure of Triumphs' jar is a great idea that really worked for me in encouraging positive behaviours and building a strong sense of community in the classroom. I found that when children and I awarded coloured gems for kindness, persistence and teamwork, it reinforced positive actions and encouraged peer recognition and support. Setting a collective goal kept children motivated and celebrating with a class reward when the jar was full created a real sense of achievement for everyone. This simple system made a big impact, helping children appreciate each other's efforts and thus strengthening our classroom culture.

In Summary: Weaving Together the Threads of Our Educational Performance

In summary, the energy you feel the moment you step into a thriving Early Years setting is unmistakable; you can feel it in the air. It's the kind of success I wish I could bottle; EYFS magic! It all begins with strong, nurturing relationships, where harmony prevails (most of the time), consistency brings reassurance and the children, and staff, are joyfully engaged.

Ultimately, the relationships you nurture with children are the culmination of all the efforts invested in building strong staff dynamics and parent partnerships. They are the final, yet most critical act that ties the entire production together. When the cast – staff, parents and children – are connected through deep and supportive relationships, the stage is set for an extraordinary performance.

Key Takeaways

Cultivating Strong Relationships for a Thriving Early Years Setting

- **Start as a team every day:** Begin each day with a quick, focused morning huddle to review the schedule, share updates and discuss specific needs or goals for each child. Use this time to establish a shared understanding of responsibilities, such as playground duties, outdoor activities, or supporting individual children. Keep it brief but meaningful, just 5–10 minutes. Rotating roles ensures every team member is engaged in all aspects of the provision, gaining a comprehensive understanding of the children's development and building a stronger, more cohesive team.
- **Build a shared vision:** A shared vision is the foundation of a unified team. Clearly and regularly communicate the child-centred goals and values of your Early Years setting, involving all staff in the process from the start. This might include an induction for new staff or regular refreshers throughout the year. Embed pedagogy and curriculum 'drivers' into this vision, ensuring alignment with the needs of your current cohort and community. For example, a focus on *oracy and communication* can empower children with the language skills to express themselves confidently, while a *real-world learning* driver can create meaningful, hands-on experiences that connect classroom learning to life beyond school. Regularly revisit and refine your vision through rich team discussions, adapting to new challenges and opportunities creating a collective sense of purpose.
- **Prioritise staff well-being:** A thriving team starts with staff who feel valued, supported and empowered. Tackle common challenges such as workload pressures and a dip in morale through proactive, practical and solution-focused

(Continued)

approaches that promote a culture of mutual respect and collaboration. Celebrate achievements through formal recognition or simple gestures like 'thank-you' shoutouts or mentions in a newsletter. Invest in professional development opportunities tailored to your team's needs and ensure staff have time to reflect and grow. Build in systems like shared schedules or rotational duties to ensure equitable workloads. Remember that happy, supported staff create a stable and nurturing environment for children.

- **Communicate with respect and openness:** Effective communication is at the heart of a strong team. Foster a culture of open dialogue where everyone feels heard and valued. Hold regular check-ins, whether through morning briefings, end-of-day reflections or regular informal conversations. Use positive language, active listening and constructive feedback to build trust. By ensuring that everyone's voice is included, you create a collaborative and transparent work environment where ideas and concerns can be freely shared.
- **Engage parents as partners:** Parents are a vital part of school life, and while partnerships take time to build, they bring lasting benefits for children. Strengthen home–school partnerships through regular communication, whether it's newsletters, online platforms or a quick chat at drop-off and pick-up. Offering practical workshops on topics like literacy or child development can give parents useful strategies to support learning at home. To remove barriers to engagement, consider flexible options like translated materials, short recorded videos or virtual meetings. Building trust and welcoming parents into school life whenever possible creates a strong bond between home and school, enriching every child's development. Side by side, we succeed.
- **Celebrate diversity and inclusion:** Welcome the rich tapestry of different cultures and backgrounds that make your setting something truly special. Why not bring families together to share their traditions and stories, creating moments of connection and joy? When children witness their own heritage reflected in their classroom, whether through the stories they read, the songs they sing, or the celebrations they become immersed in, learning becomes purposeful. Acknowledging birthdays, cherished traditions and family milestones sends a powerful message: you belong here. True inclusivity should not be an add-on; these moments are the heartbeat of a thriving community, where every story matters and every child shines.
- **Enhance peer relationships:** Facilitate activities that promote peer collaboration, like group projects or child-friendly team-building exercises. Teach children conflict resolution skills and model empathy, patience and active listening. Introduce buddy systems or rotating leadership roles to encourage responsibility and mutual support. By creating an environment where children feel safe to express themselves and build connections, you help them develop critical interpersonal skills that will serve them throughout their lives.
- **Focus on reflective practices:** Reflection is key to continuous improvement. Encourage staff to regularly assess their practices through journals, team

discussions or relevant action research. Use feedback from peers, parents and even the children to identify areas for development. Incorporate tools like video recordings and shared observations to analyse interactions and highlight successes. Focus on one aspect of practice at a time, making incremental changes that have a significant impact within your setting. Making time for reflection not only nurtures individual growth but also deepens the heart of your setting, strengthening the way everyone learns, works and connects.

- **Empower children's voices:** We know that building strong, trusting relationships with children is essential. Take time early on to understand their unique personalities, interests and needs. Practice deep listening, truly hearing their thoughts and emotions and use their passions to shape learning activities. Offer genuine praise that acknowledges their effort and individuality, reinforcing their sense of self-worth. Valuing children's voices helps them grow in confidence and feel a deep connection to those around them.
- **Foster community connections:** Extend learning beyond the classroom and right into the heart of the community. Build strong connections with local organisations and cultural institutions, bringing real-world experiences to life. Invite families and the wider community to join in the joy of learning alongside you, through cultural celebrations, charity drives and shared moments of discovery. Encourage children to take an active role in community projects, e.g. library events or sporting activities, cultivating a sense of belonging, responsibility and great pride. When education reaches beyond your school walls, it becomes richer, more inclusive, more relevant and filled with meaningful connections, supporting children's development as active, caring citizens.

References

Clinton, H. (1996) *It Takes a Village: And Other Lessons Children Teach Us*. New York: Simon & Schuster.

Department for Education (DfE) (2021a) *Birth to 5 Matters*.

Department for Education (DfE) (2021b) *Working in Partnership with Parents and Carers*. Available at: https://help-for-early-years-providers.education.gov.uk/support-for-practitioners/working-in-partnership-with-parents-and-carers

Early Education (2021) *Birth to 5 Matters: Non-statutory Guidance for the Early Years Foundation Stage*. Available at: https://birthto5matters.org.uk/parents-as-partners/

3
Lights, Camera, Action
Crafting a Magical Environment

In the last chapter, we explored the profound impact of strong relationships within the Early Years and how these really can shape a child's world. Now, in Chapter 3, we step into the beating heart of where those essential connections take root and soar: the Early Years classroom.

Like a beautifully crafted theatre set on opening night, the classroom is an exciting invitation to explore, to create and to wonder. For a Reception child, this space is their world; an alluring stage where every day brings new discoveries that spark joy, curiosity and a deep sense of belonging. Within these motivational walls, learning comes to life, scene by scene, moment by moment, as children grow in confidence, build resilience and revel in the excitement of discovering what lies ahead.

An Early Years classroom is so much more than furniture and fixtures; it's a world carefully shaped to spark curiosity and joy. The layout, the colours, the spaces available, the way resources are placed, whisper an open invitation to explore. A space designed with thought and purpose ignites intrigue for children. It lures them in, urging them to engage, to experiment, to take risks, to be themselves and to make their own discoveries. In such a setting, learning is something children claim for themselves, with wide eyes, eager hands and a growing thirst to know more.

Designing an effective and attractive learning environment can initially feel overwhelming. The true reality is that most educators are working within tight constraints, whether it's budget limitations, space restrictions or the resources available. While an unlimited budget (or any budget) would certainly make things easier, teachers often need to make the most of what they already have. Countless times, I've walked into a classroom, new or familiar, and felt dazed by either the abundance or lack of resources, and then faced the enormous task of creating an inspiring space that works for my eager new starters. My goal has always been to design a room that flows naturally, sparking curiosity for all children with just the right balance of stimulation.

Even when you think you've 'nailed it' and have all the areas perfectly set up, two days in you realise the construction area is far too small and the children are gravitating towards arts and crafts more than anything else! An ever-evolving approach to classroom layout is key; adjustments within the first few days are inevitable as you observe how children use the space. That said, it's essential to establish a sense of stability early on. Consistency in the layout promotes independence; when children know where to find what they need, they develop agency, taking ownership of their learning and thriving in their own domains. Therefore, your classroom should strike a balance between offering consistency and introducing new experiences. The goal is to implement gradual, subtle changes over time rather than making drastic shifts all at once. These enhancements introduce new challenges, intrigue, motivation and opportunities for development, guiding children through progressive stages of learning. For instance, transitioning from Duplo to Lego provides a more intricate building experience, helping children refine their fine motor skills and problem-solving abilities. Similarly, adding watercolours to the art area can nurture more advanced painting techniques, encouraging experimentation with colour mixing and creativity. These thoughtful upgrades ensure that the environment evolves alongside the children's growing abilities, promoting continuous learning and skill development across the seven areas of learning.

Creating the ideal classroom isn't about following a set formula – there isn't one; it's about shaping the space to work for you *and* your children, where learning flows naturally and each child feels safe and empowered to explore, create and thrive.

Your Unique Space

You, your cohort of children and your classroom space is unique. Professional judgement regarding classroom set up is crucial, particularly when considering the specific needs of your children. If your class includes children who may benefit from a calmer environment, adjustments should be made accordingly. Factors such as class size, seating arrangements, learning areas and individual needs must all be thoughtfully considered to create an environment that supports learning and growth for all learners. The goal is to strike a perfect balance between aesthetics, practicality and children's engagement.

Every teacher has a unique style and personality, which will inevitably be reflected in their classroom setup. It's your room, with your resources, most of which you have probably bought yourself! Personal touches make the classroom more welcoming and engaging for children, helping to build stronger connections. The flow of the classroom should work for you as well as the children. Whether it's having a base or desk, designating specific areas to storage or creating organisational zones for the whole EYFS team to contribute to, ensuring everything is in place helps the space function smoothly and supports both you and the children in the long term.

There's a popular belief among some influencers that classrooms should be minimalist, with neutral tones, carefully curated wooden shelving and baskets of natural materials. This sounds idyllic! However, not all educators have access to these resources and it's important to work within the limits of your specific context. As an advocate for creating engaging spaces, I believe a well-designed classroom balances calm and order with vibrant elements, creating a dynamic flow that nurtures both focus and creativity. When the space reflects the energy of the children, it becomes more than a room; it becomes an environment where learning comes alive. Selecting materials that are relevant and engaging, while ensuring a balance between stimulation and calm, helps maintain an environment conducive to learning.

Research from the University of Salford's HEAD project (Barrett et al. 2015) found that a well-designed classroom can significantly boost learning outcomes. Their study suggested that classrooms with neutral walls and occasional splashes of colour can enhance children's progress by up to 16% over a year. The research emphasises the balance between too much and too little stimulation, suggesting that moderate displays and highlighted walls against calm backgrounds are most effective. Peter Barrett, leader of the project, said 'There are low levels of learning when the environment is under-stimulated, and low levels when it is over-stimulated. It is right at the mid-point – when you have a highlighted wall against a calm background, or plain walls with an occasional splash of colour – that you get the best result' (Barratt et al. 2015). John Coe, chair of the National Association for Primary Education, supports this view, advocating for a balanced setup, 'neither over-stimulating nor unduly calming', that enhances learning affordably while keeping children's needs central (University of Salford 2015). These quotes emphasise the need for balance in classroom design. An under-stimulated environment can result in lack of engagement for learners, while an over-stimulated one can cause unneeded distraction. The ideal setup combines calm surroundings with intentional pops of colour or highlights, creating a space that fosters both focus and creativity.

Therefore, contrary to the belief that colour should be avoided like the plague, research reveals that *some* colour *can* greatly enhance learning experiences but, I agree that it's best to be mindful here (and very demure). Warm colours like yellow and orange can uplift mood and boost engagement, much like the positive effects of a sunny day. Meanwhile, 'a well-designed classroom that uses "calming and neutral colours, like blues and greens" can help students feel more relaxed and focused, reducing distractions and enhancing concentration' (Eslit 2020). This finding underscores the importance of colour in creating an optimal learning environment, balancing stimulation with calm to support effective engagement. It's a matter of subtlety; just don't go over the top! I must agree wholeheartedly with Adoniou (2017), who asserts that 'highly decorated classrooms are more of a distraction than an aid to learning'. She insists that 'we need a happy compromise' (Adoniou 2017). Yes, I'll admit it: I've spent time and resources creating elaborate role-play areas in the past, believing they fully engaged the children. However, I've come to respect the growing body of research from recent years, which shows that these setups can actually lead to overstimulation and distraction for young learners.

Practical Tips 3.1

Creating an Engaging and Calming Learning Space in a Balanced Classroom

1. **Avoiding overstimulation:** Colour plays a role, but it's the overall environment that matters. While bright colours can bring energy, they work best in moderation. A feature wall or a carefully chosen pop of colour here and there can create a focal point but too much visual noise, be that walls crammed with displays, resources squeezed into every corner or untidy classroom zones, can be overwhelming. Arrange colourful furniture strategically to maintain a balanced visual appeal. Use storage solutions to minimise clutter and create a tidy environment. Thoughtful, uncluttered spaces help children focus, feel calm and truly engage with their learning environment.

2. **Enhancing accessibility:** Position materials and resources at child-friendly heights, ensuring all children can access learning tools independently. Low shelves and open storage containers make it easier for children to engage actively with their environment, fostering confidence and self-direction. Involving the children in setting up displays and areas fosters a sense of ownership, responsibility and connection, helping them feel that the classroom belongs to them as much as to their teacher.

3. **Creating visual flow:** Use visual markers, such as low dividers or shelving units, to separate different activity zones. This subtle guidance can help children understand the purpose of each space while maintaining a calm, organised classroom flow that minimises distractions and promotes focus.

4. **Incorporating learning resources:** Use educational resources thoughtfully to create a learning environment that is both interactive and visually engaging, without overwhelming the space. Choose resources that directly support key learning objectives and display them in an organised, inviting way. Designate specific areas for certain resources to encourage hands-on exploration, while keeping other spaces clearer to avoid visual clutter. Learning spaces that are engaging don't require extravagant spending. Simple organisation, child-friendly displays and thoughtful colour use can help create a functional, budget-friendly classroom.

5. **Incorporating natural elements and personal touches:** Adding plants or nature-inspired decor can improve air quality and create a calming atmosphere, enhancing children's focus and well-being. Research suggests that natural elements in classrooms help reduce stress and increase engagement, contributing to a more supportive learning environment (University of Salford 2015). Adding your personal stamp to the space will make it more inviting, creating a warm, welcoming atmosphere that strengthens connections. Every teacher brings something unique so it's important that the classroom environment works for you too.

Creating a balanced classroom environment with thoughtful use of colour and personal touches can transform learning spaces. Embrace the resources you have, add hints of colour and ensure the classroom is clutter-free and not overstimulating. It's wrong to believe all classrooms should look the same and be bland; colour isn't the enemy here. A well-designed classroom reflects the unique style of the teacher and supports a positive, engaging learning experience for the children.

Selecting resources for an Early Years setting also requires careful thought to ensure they are inclusive, diverse and representative of all children. Thoughtfully chosen props and materials allow children to engage in play that reflects their own identities and promotes an understanding of different cultures and experiences.

Liz Pemberton, an anti-racist trainer and consultant known as *The Black Nursery Manager*, emphasises this importance, stating that early childhood settings should 'embrace all children's racial, cultural and religious backgrounds' to foster a sense of belonging. She further highlights that 'everybody working with small children must recognise the significant impact they have on their worldview', underscoring the role educators play in shaping inclusive environments that celebrate diversity and encourage open conversations about identity and inclusion (Pemberton n.d.). Pemberton advocates for thoughtful, non-gendered and culturally inclusive materials that invite children to explore diversity and see their own identities reflected in their learning environment (Pemberton 2022a; Pemberton 2022b).

Classroom Organisation for Maximum Learning – Areas or Zones

An inclusive classroom design ensures that the environment caters to the physical, sensory and cognitive needs of all children. This might include using low shelves for easy access to materials, clearly labelled resources and designated sensory areas with calming textures and sounds. Consider the layout in terms of clear pathways for movement, especially for children with physical needs and the availability of sensory-friendly spaces where children can go to self-regulate. Ensuring that all children feel comfortable and have free access to the resources fosters independence and confidence in their learning.

Research from the University of Salford highlights that 'the most powerful impact is made by the physical design of the particular classroom in which [children] spend such a vitally important time with their teacher', emphasising how thoughtful classroom design can significantly boost engagement and learning (University of Salford 2015). The way furniture is arranged can significantly impact how children engage with the environment and each other. Of course, this really does depend on the space that you have available. Where possible, it's helpful to create small, well-defined learning areas within the classroom to foster movement, interaction and collaboration. For instance, a cosy reading corner with soft seating can promote independent or quiet group reading, while a corner with tables and various materials encourages hands-on creativity and problem-solving. Clearly separating these areas allows children to choose activities that match their interests and needs, supporting a range of passions and interests.

> **Well-Defined Learning Areas (Indoor)**
> - A book area and/or cosy reading nooks with soft seating, ideal for quiet, independent reading or small group story time.
> - A construction area with building blocks, train tracks or other materials to foster creativity, problem-solving and fine motor skills. Ample space is required here.
> - A home corner and/or role-play area where children can engage in imaginative play, enhancing social skills and empathy.
> - An arts and crafts area equipped with an array of materials and tools for drawing, painting and hands-on creativity.
> - You may have a designated writing area equipped with ample resources to inspire mark making and writing. This is great, although I would also ensure that writing opportunities are everywhere!
> - A maths area can provide a dedicated space with hands-on resources to explore number, shape, space and measures through play. This is valuable, though I would also ensure that maths is woven throughout all areas of the environment!
> - Sand and water play areas engage children's sensory exploration and help develop early scientific concepts such as volume, flow and material properties. In my experience, due to limited classroom space, I've often placed the sand and water areas outside.

Apart from these defined zones, everything else truly depends on the space available in your classroom. In my opinion, investigation and discovery shouldn't be confined to one corner; it should flow naturally throughout the classroom, encouraging children to explore and question everything around them. If space allows, creating a dedicated 'small world' area is invaluable for developing communication and language skills. With elements like dollshouses, mini figures or farmyard sets, children can engage in role-play and storytelling, which fosters creativity and vocabulary growth.

The key is to make the most of whatever space you have. If your room is spacious, you can create larger, more distinct areas, or even incorporate multiple areas to provide varied experiences for the children. However, if space is limited, flexibility is essential. Consider combining areas or rotating materials and resources to ensure the classroom remains dynamic and engaging without feeling overcrowded. Ultimately, the layout should support children's independent learning while maximising the space you have. As *Birth to 5 Matters* reminds us, 'Children are unique and holistic learners, thriving within environments that support their individual and diverse motivations, interests and needs.' They flourish when offered 'a wealth of possibilities within varied contexts,' particularly in 'stimulating and challenging environments that value exploration and play' (Early Years Coalition 2021). Tailoring the space to these principles ensures that children's interests and curiosities drive their learning.

> **Ten Key Questions for EYFS Practitioners to Ask when Planning their Classroom Layout and Learning Zones**
>
> - How does my layout support independent access to resources?
> - Are the learning areas clearly defined and purposeful?
> - Is there a balance between open-ended play opportunities and structured activities?
> - Can the layout adapt easily to different activities and needs?
> - Does the environment encourage sensory exploration and engagement?
> - How does the layout promote communication and language development?
> - Does the classroom cater to various learning approaches, interests and abilities?
> - Does the layout support both group collaboration and individual work?
> - How does my layout ensure the safety and well-being of the children while allowing them to explore independently?
> - Have I created spaces for quiet reflection and self-regulation, supporting children's emotional well-being?

Think of the classroom areas like the subtle shifts in lighting or stage props in a theatre; small nuances that gently guide children's thinking and open creative pathways for exploration. Just as a director might introduce a new prop to capture the audience's attention, you can introduce gentle prompts through carefully selected enhancements, sowing the seeds of curiosity and wonder. For example, a simple addition to the small world area, such as a miniature animal or a new texture, can spark new stories and perspectives.

Reading Area

The reading area is so much more than just a corner for books; it's a gateway to imagination, exploration and discovery. Reading opens the door to new worlds, expanding children's vocabulary, developing their language skills and fostering a lifelong love for stories. A thoughtfully designed reading area offers comfort, nurtures creativity and promotes literacy, becoming the heart of the classroom where young minds can flourish and grow through the magic of storytelling.

> **Practical Tips 3.2**
>
> Inspiring Young Readers by Creating a Reading Oasis
>
> 1. **Create a cosy haven:** Use soft seating like cushions, bean bags or a small sofa or armchair to make the reading area feel like a warm, inviting retreat where children can lose themselves in a book. A space that feels safe and nurturing encourages a deeper connection to stories. Use soft rugs or natural dividers to create a dedicated space that is calm and peaceful. In this tranquil nook, children can escape into their stories, free from distractions.
>
> *(Continued)*

2. **Accessible magic:** Make sure books are stored at child-height on low-level shelves, empowering children to independently explore the magical worlds hidden in books. Let them feel the excitement of choosing their next adventure all on their own. Ensure there's enough room for children to gather for a group story time, where shared stories build a sense of community and joy. These moments of togetherness can ignite a collective love for reading that resonates with each child. Display featured books that change regularly, sparking curiosity and encouraging children to discover new adventures. The excitement of fresh texts keeps the space dynamic and engaging.
3. **Books that spark joy:** Curate a mix of books; bright picture books, interactive stories, and ones with characters that resonate with the children. A well-chosen book has the power to ignite imagination and wonder, inviting children into the narrative. Allow children to contribute their own stories or drawings to the space, making it feel personal.
4. **Interactive storytelling:** Incorporate storytelling props like puppets or story bags that bring books to life, transforming a quiet reading session into an interactive experience. This creates a sense of magic, where children can become part of the story.
5. **Natural light, natural curiosity:** Position the reading area by a window to bathe the space in natural light, creating a serene atmosphere that draws children in. Natural elements provide comfort and encourage mindfulness while reading.
6. **Visual story inspirations:** Add splashes of inspiration with posters or art that reflect beloved book characters or quotes that celebrate the magic of reading. These visuals subtly encourage children to delve deeper into the stories they see around them.

Reading Nooks

Creating reading opportunities throughout the learning environment encourages children to engage with books naturally during different activities and play. Reading doesn't have to be confined to one area. By integrating books and stories into various spaces throughout your classroom, children are more likely to encounter stories that spark their interest and imagination. Here are some ideas for book nooks that can be spread across the setting to promote a love of reading:

Practical Tips 3.3

Sparking a Love for Stories with Creative Reading Nooks

1. **Book baskets:** Place small baskets filled with books in different play areas, such as near the home corner, construction area or outdoor play area, so children can access stories related to their play activities.

2. **Treasure chests of books:** Use a decorative treasure chest to hold books about pirates, adventures or exploration. Children can 'discover' these hidden books during free play, encouraging imaginative reading.
3. **Mini displays based on children's interests:** Create small displays that showcase books aligned with children's current fascinations, such as dinosaurs, space or animals. This personalised approach will draw children in and make reading a natural extension of their interests.
4. **Reading dens:** Set up cosy reading dens using canopies, blankets or pop-up tents. These small, enclosed spaces offer a sense of privacy and can be stocked with themed books for children to explore in a quiet, comfortable setting. Add torches too for extra excitement!
5. **Under-table book nooks:** Convert the space under tables into mini reading nooks with cushions and book baskets, offering a hidden spot where children can read quietly to each other.
6. **Themed reading corners:** For example, near a small world play area, include books that expand on the theme, such as farm animals or fairytales. This encourages children to combine role-play with storytelling. Use a rolling cart with books that can be moved around the classroom or setting. Children can explore stories wherever they happen to be and you can change the selection regularly to keep it fresh.

Construction Area

The construction area is an exciting and dynamic space where children can unleash their creativity, explore problem-solving and build vital motor skills. It's where young minds work together to create structures, solve challenges and develop spatial awareness. As the year progresses, this area can evolve from simple block play to more complex builds, incorporating new materials and tools that expand learning and ignite even more curiosity and determination. Here's how you can set up and enhance the construction area to engage children throughout the year:

Practical Tips 3.4

Creating an Engaging Construction Area for Collaborative Play

1. **Start simple, build confidence:** Begin with basic building blocks and materials, allowing children to develop confidence in their construction abilities. Encourage them to experiment with stacking, balancing and connecting, fostering early problem-solving skills.

(Continued)

2. **Introduce new materials over time:** As the year progresses, gradually introduce more diverse materials such as ramps, pulleys, wooden planks and connectors. These additions will challenge children to think more critically and explore basic engineering concepts.
3. **Incorporate loose parts:** Offer loose parts like tubes, corks or pieces of fabric that can be integrated into their constructions, promoting open-ended play and imaginative building.
4. **Teamwork and collaboration:** As children grow more comfortable, encourage collaborative builds where they can work together to create larger structures. This fosters teamwork, communication and shared problem-solving. Create a display area where children's constructions can be showcased, validating their efforts and inspiring others along the way.
5. **Blueprints and planning:** As the year progresses, challenge children to draw simple blueprints of their designs, teaching early planning skills and allowing them to map out their ideas before constructing.
6. **Real-life inspirations:** Introduce books, photos and videos of real-world structures like bridges, towers and homes to inspire children to model their constructions on things they see in the world around them. Include diverse and culturally representative materials, such as small figurines, miniature buildings or architectural elements from various cultures. This allows children to incorporate different cultural styles and structures into their creations, promoting inclusivity and helping children see themselves and others represented in their play.

Home Corner/Role-Play

The home corner and role-play area are essential spaces in the EYFS setting, encouraging creativity, social skills and imaginative play. These areas provide children with opportunities to explore real-life scenarios and engage in collaborative play, encouraging rich and purposeful communication. They mimic, negotiate, and create, immersing themselves in imagined experiences that hold real developmental value. These spaces nurture creativity, strengthen social bonds, and encourage rich, purposeful language. Over time, these spaces can evolve to reflect the children's interests, introducing new themes and props to deepen their learning experiences. As the EYFS framework reminds us, 'play is essential for children's development, building their confidence as they learn to explore, relate to others, set their own goals and solve problems' (Department for Education 2024). In these thoughtfully planned spaces, play becomes the vehicle for deep learning, shaping how children think, relate, and make sense of the world around them.

Practical Tips 3.5

Inspiring Imaginative Play with a Home Corner Haven

1. **Home corner setup:** The home corner acts as a foundation for imaginative play, where children can role-play familiar scenarios, like family life or caregiving. It provides comfort and encourages children to express themselves in a safe, relatable context.
2. **Start with familiar elements:** Begin with basic furniture like a kitchen, table and baby care items to represent a welcoming home environment. Including items from various cultural backgrounds, like traditional cooking tools or decorations, helps all children see their experiences reflected and feel more connected as they role-play everyday activities.
3. **Real-life, culturally inclusive props:** Introduce real-life props gradually, such as utensils, pots, pans and empty food containers that are familiar across diverse cultures. Items like chopsticks, spice jars or small cultural artifacts from around the world add authenticity and allow children to explore problem-solving and cooperation while experiencing elements of other cultures.
4. **Community requests:** Invite parents to contribute items from home that can enrich the play area, often with the motto 'your trash is our treasure'. Simple items like empty food packaging, fabric scraps or small artifacts from their culture can add authenticity and diversity to the home corner. This approach encourages family involvement and provides children with relatable, everyday items that reflect their backgrounds, making the space even more meaningful and inclusive. Also write to local businesses, as many are willing to support schools by donating resources.
5. **Add themes based on interests and identities:** Throughout the year, adapt the home corner to match children's interests and backgrounds. Include elements like a doctor's kit, shopping baskets or gardening tools, along with culturally representative play items like traditional clothing, books or holiday decorations. This keeps the space dynamic, inclusive and familiar, allowing children to explore roles from a variety of cultural perspectives.
6. **Encourage language development with inclusive props:** Provide props that encourage communication, such as telephones, menus or signs in multiple languages to represent the classroom community. This supports conversation, storytelling and vocabulary growth, allowing children to build language skills and recognise the value of linguistic and cultural diversity.

Additional Role-Play Area Setup (If Space Allows)

A dedicated role-play area opens doors to both familiar and new worlds. Here, they become shopkeepers, astronauts, chefs or safari explorers, negotiating, delegating and problem solving as they go. Through role-play, children act out stories and real-world scenarios, using language in exciting and meaningful ways. I have loved watching children over the years as they step into different roles with such joy and conviction. One moment a caring nurse, the next a daring explorer; children's imaginations know no bounds and through role-play I've seen them soar in confidence and find their voices in ways that are truly magical. Sometimes the simplest additions spark the richest play – let children take the lead ... and watch imagination do the rest.

> ### Practical Tips 3.6
> ### Creating an Inclusive and Engaging Role-Play Area
>
> 1. **Involve children in planning:** Ask children what themes they are interested in and use their ideas to design the role-play areas in the classroom. Themes could range from a post office to a hospital, catering to their current fascinations and making the space even more meaningful. I loved asking the children for ideas and their excitement and creativity never ceased to amaze me. If you lack the space, then simply have role-play nooks. A doctor's kit and x rays in one space and a makeshift dashboard of a space shuttle in another. They are provocations and don't have to be too realistic – the children will do the rest. A cardboard box is sometimes enough!
> 2. **Provide diverse props:** Offering a variety of props encourages role-play that's imaginative, diverse and free from gender stereotypes. Items like costumes, play money, tickets, cooking utensils and tools foster creative problem-solving and deepen children's engagement in play.
> 3. **Gender-neutral:** To ensure the space is welcoming and inclusive, consider providing props that are neutral and open-ended, allowing children to explore roles without reinforcing traditional gender expectations. For example, include items like aprons, construction hats, doctor's kits and gardening tools in various colours and designs so all children feel represented and free to explore any role.
> 4. **Enhance the atmosphere with sound and lighting:** Add sensory elements like ambient sounds and soft lighting to bring role-play themes to life. For example, include office sounds with phones ringing, rainforest sounds with bird calls or underwater sounds for an ocean theme. These sensory elements create an immersive experience that stimulates children's senses, enriching their imaginative play and enhancing engagement.
> 5. **Fostering imaginative play:** Both home corners and role-play areas support creative development by giving children the freedom to express themselves, act out familiar scenarios and invent new ones. Through role-play, children practice and expand their communication and language skills, using new vocabulary, storytelling and dialogue as they act out roles. Role-play areas naturally lead to collaboration and teamwork as children negotiate roles, take turns and work together to act out scenarios, supporting their personal, social and emotional development.

Arts and Craft Area

The arts and craft area is the hub of creative expression in an Early Years setting. It's a place where children are free to explore materials, experiment without rigid formulas and develop fine motor skills as they bring their imaginations to life. This space isn't just about producing 'pretty' artwork; it's where children can make choices, take creative risks and experiment with ideas in an open-ended, skill-building environment. The art area bursts with possibilities, inviting children to dive into a world of colour, texture and imagination. It's a space where creativity knows no limits; where bold ideas take shape, tiny hands transform blank pages into masterpieces and every brushstroke builds confidence in self-expression.

Practical Tips 3.7

Crafting a Vibrant and Inclusive Art Area to Ignite Creativity and Expression

1. **Open-ended materials:** Provide a variety of materials such as paper, fabric scraps, recycled items, glue, different-sized brushes, printing materials and paints. Open-ended resources encourage children to explore without predetermined outcomes, fostering creativity and critical thinking. Introduce art challenges based on classroom themes, seasons or children's interests. For example, a nature-inspired art project using leaves, twigs and stones can connect children to the natural world around them. Ensure the space allows for both structured and free art time. Some children may enjoy following simple instructions for creating something specific inspired by an artist, while others thrive in an open-ended creative space where they can express themselves freely.
2. **Easily accessible supplies:** Organise materials on low shelves in labelled baskets so children can independently select what they need. Introducing new textures, colours and exciting tools throughout the year will spark curiosity and encourage children to push their creative boundaries, building both skill and confidence. If space allows, create specific stations for particular activities, such as a painting station, a clay table or a cutting and sticking area.
3. **Inspirational displays:** Hang posters, photos or books that showcase famous artwork or creative processes. These visuals can provide great inspiration and give children ideas on how to use the materials available to them. Talk about the work of different artists often and why not invite some local artists into your setting to work alongside the children.
4. **Process over product:** Focus on the creative process rather than the end result. Allow children to experiment freely with different techniques and materials without the pressure of making something 'perfect'. Celebrate their exploration

(Continued)

and curiosity. However, it's also crucial to introduce new skills, such as printing techniques, shading, colour mixing and blending as some children will love learning new approaches. By modelling new and exciting skills, children will naturally feel inspired to experiment and integrate them into their own work, using them in innovative and independent ways.

5   **Provide different surfaces:** Offer a range of surfaces for children to work on, such as easels, tables, outdoor walls, chalkboards and even the floor. Providing different surfaces encourages children to explore creativity from various angles and perspectives, promoting both physical engagement and imaginative thinking. By working on a vertical easel, for example, children improve upper body strength and hand–eye coordination, while working on the floor offers freedom for large-scale expression.

6   **Display children's work:** Create a gallery or display wall where children can showcase their marvellous creations. This not only boosts self-esteem but also inspires other children to experiment and try new techniques. A simple washing line on a wall at child height works particularly well, as it allows children to take ownership of their display, making the work accessible and visible to them. Or even a low display board would work. This encourages them to feel proud of their achievements and motivates them to continue exploring their creativity.

Writing Areas

As Voltaire once expressed, 'Writing is the painting of the voice' (Voltaire n.d.), capturing the power of words to evoke imagery, emotion and thought. Just as a painter uses colours and shapes to communicate creative ideas, emotions and personal stories, young writers use letters and words to bring their inner worlds to life. Encouraging a love for writing in early childhood unlocks a world of imagination and expression, laying a strong foundation for future learning. A love for writing, nurtured from the very beginning, gives children the courage to put their thoughts into the world and the power to make their mark. Writing should feel magical. The joy of crafting a message, creating a story or labelling their work should spark the same excitement as reading a favourite book. Writing must be woven into everyday experiences so children come to see it as a natural and enjoyable part of their world.

Writing opportunities should be embedded throughout your provision rather than confined to a single 'area'. Integrating writing opportunities 'everywhere' creates a literacy-rich environment where writing becomes a natural and integral part of *all* activities. This approach encourages children to see writing as a valuable tool for communication and expression across various contexts. It also enhances their fine motor skills, promotes creativity and supports the development of writing skills in a variety of meaningful ways.

Practical Tips 3.8

Encouraging a Passion for Writing and a Love for Expression

1. **Incorporate writing throughout your provision:** Writing should be a seamless part of children's play throughout the classroom. Provide clipboards, pens, pencils and notepads in every area, whether it's the construction, role-play or outdoor area, so that writing becomes a natural and integrated activity. This approach encourages children to see writing as an essential tool for documenting their ideas, adding details to their play and communicating with others, making it an organic part of their daily routine.
2. **Buckets of writing tools:** Scatter buckets filled with pens, pencils, crayons, chalks and markers across the classroom. This makes writing materials easily accessible and encourages spontaneous writing during free play.
3. **Writing belts or caddies:** Equip children with writing belts or caddies containing small notebooks and pens, allowing them to carry their writing tools wherever they go. This encourages spontaneous mark-making, list-making and storytelling as part of their play. A police officer might jot down clues and issue 'tickets,' a shopkeeper could take customer orders or write receipts, and an explorer might sketch maps or record discoveries. Journalists can capture 'breaking news', vets can log animal check-ups, and construction workers can draft blueprints or take measurements. With writing always at their fingertips, children naturally begin to see it as a meaningful and essential part of their world!
4. **Clipboards and writing frames:** Provide clipboards with simple writing frames or templates that give children a sense of purpose, like themed writing paper for story retells, menu cards in the role-play kitchen or invitations in the home corner. Offer blank booklets or notepads too that children can use to create their own stories, journals or comic strips. These open-ended formats encourage creativity and allow children to become authors of their own little books.
5. **Lined paper, Post-it notes and envelopes:** Having lined paper and envelopes readily available lets children write letters to their peers and family members, adding an element of excitement to communication. Post-it notes can be used for labelling creations, making lists or sending quick messages to friends in a well-resourced message centre. For further insights into the power of message centres in Early Years settings, Greg Bottrill's work provides valuable research and practical strategies (Bottrill 2018).
6. **Real reasons to write:** Provide children with a variety of opportunities and real reasons to write, so that writing becomes a natural, purposeful part of their day. EYFS staff should model writing at every opportunity, as children are captivated by the excitement adults show when they write. They can write thank you cards, get well soon notes and invitations to school events, or even post letters home

(Continued)

> to family members. Encourage them to create signs for their constructions, write recipes in the home corner, design event promotion posters, make shopping lists, send messages to friends or record discoveries in a nature journal. When writing is embedded in real experiences, children see it as an essential tool for communication, creativity and connection.

Classroom Displays, Wonder Walls

A well-designed classroom display serves as a visual extension of learning, celebrating both children's achievements and their ongoing learning journeys. While bold, colourful displays can spark engagement, there's a growing preference for a more minimalist approach, where less is more. By focusing on clarity and purpose, displays can encourage reflection and deeper thinking without overwhelming the senses.

Although I've created vibrant displays in the past (and still would occasionally), I now lean towards using hessian backdrops, which provide a neutral, calming canvas. This simple foundation allows the children's work to shine, showcasing their creativity and progress in an understated but powerful way. It's also highly durable and low-maintenance, saving valuable time while maintaining a polished, long-lasting display. You can add a splash of colour with an innovative border such as children's handprints or gathered streamers.

Misty Adoniou, Associate Professor in Language, Literacy and TESL, University of Canberra, believes that 'displays designed to reinforce, remind or support learning should be co-constructed with the children, in the context of learning – not simply appear on the walls after yet another teacher's weekend sacrificed to the laminating machine' (Adoniou 2017). Involving children in the decorating process remains key. When children contribute their own work to the displays, they feel a stronger connection to the classroom. Child-created projects and artwork, when thoughtfully integrated, reflect their interests and learning journeys, transforming the classroom into a dynamic and evolving space that grows with their progress.

Sarah Wright, senior lecturer at Edge Hill University states that 'yes, you want to "wow" your new class with their beautiful learning environment, but you have to remember that it belongs to them as much as to you. Your classroom needs to grow along with your children' (Wright 2016). Wright's comment emphasises a fundamental aspect of classroom design; ownership and agency for the children. While it's important to create a welcoming and inspiring environment, the space should evolve with the children. Encouraging them to contribute to the environment fosters a sense of belonging and responsibility.

Sensory Experiences: Engaging All the Senses

Engaging young children through their senses, touch, sound, smell, sight, and even taste, can significantly enhance their learning experiences. A multi-sensory environment taps into children's natural curiosity and supports deeper cognitive development by offering varied stimuli. Think of the classroom as a theatre stage, where each sensory element acts as a prop, subtly guiding children's focus and engagement. Sensory elements like tactile materials, calming music and aromatic scents make the learning space more inviting and interactive. For example, incorporating soft fabrics or scented herbs allows children to physically engage with their surroundings, while calming background music or sounds of nature creates a soothing atmosphere, much like a background score that sets the mood in a performance.

Children learn best through hands-on, sensory-rich activities that allow them to physically interact with their environment. Providing opportunities like sensory trays filled with materials such as rice, beans or water and nature tables with shells, rocks or plants, encourages tactile exploration. Much like a director introducing a new prop on stage to spark curiosity and imagination, the addition of new, hands-on materials invites children to explore and create. A sensory corner might include textured materials, scented playdough or interactive light displays, each acting as a key component of the 'set' that draws children deeper into the 'scene' of learning.

Incorporating sensory experiences into the classroom supports a diverse range of learning needs, creating an inclusive environment. By offering varied stimuli that engage all the senses, educators create an ever-evolving, interactive 'stage' where children can actively learn, explore and connect with their surroundings.

Outdoor Learning: Beyond Four Walls, into Endless Possibilities

In early childhood education, outdoor learning offers a magical and dynamic extension of the classroom. It should be seen as a space for adventure, discovery and problem solving and not just an outdoor version of indoor activities. Research consistently shows that outdoor play has profound benefits on early childhood development, enhancing physical health, critical thinking skills and emotional resilience. Outdoor play is also a powerful tool in developing lifelong habits of physical fitness, cognitive growth and emotional balance. As outlined in the EYFS Framework, outdoor learning supports the development of gross motor skills through activities like running, climbing and jumping, which are vital for building core strength, coordination and agility. 'Children need access to indoor and outdoor environments that help develop their gross motor skills, with you to guide and support them, every day. Outdoors is where children have the freedom to be as physical as they can be' (Department for Education: Gross Motor Skills 2025).

As Alistair Bryce-Clegg mentions, 'Outdoor play isn't an afterthought. It is a critical part of a child's development, offering experiences that can't always be replicated indoors' (Bryce-Clegg 2018). This belief reinforces the idea that the outdoor classroom isn't just an extension of indoor learning; it's a whole new world where children can grow, explore and flourish in ways that nurture both body and mind. By emphasising the significance of outdoor learning, educators provide children with the freedom to interact with nature, develop resilience and foster a deep connection with the world around them, laying the foundation for lifelong learning and well-being.

> **Practical Tips 3.9**
>
> Fostering Playful Exploration and Discovery Through Outdoor Learning
>
> 1. **Embrace sensory exploration:** Incorporate sensory-rich materials such as mud, sand, water and natural textures like leaves and pinecones. This encourages children to explore their environment, stimulating emotional regulation and cognitive development through hands-on discovery.
> 2. **Set up a mud kitchen:** A mud kitchen offers endless opportunities for imaginative play and creativity. Equip the space with old pots, pans and spoons to allow children to engage in role-play, while also exploring the textures and properties of natural materials.
> 3. **Include gardening projects:** Gardening nurtures a sense of responsibility, builds patience, and brings the life cycle of plants to life. Provide children with tools like watering cans, trowels and seeds, encouraging them to tend to their own plants, fostering environmental awareness and fine motor skill development.
> 4. **Create obstacle courses and physical challenges:** Set up obstacle courses using natural and play materials like logs, cones and tunnels. These activities help develop gross motor skills such as balance, coordination and agility, while also encouraging teamwork and perseverance.
> 5. **Use loose parts for construction:** Offer loose parts such as wooden planks, stones and fabric to encourage creative construction play. Children can build, experiment and solve problems, fostering critical thinking, collaboration and spatial awareness.
> 6. **Incorporate water play:** Water play offers a fantastic sensory experience that enhances motor skills and introduces basic science concepts like buoyancy, flow and volume. Use water trays, hoses, containers, funnels, pipes and measuring jugs to inspire curiosity and exploration.
> 7. **Introduce large-scale art:** Provide opportunities for children to engage in large-scale outdoor art projects using chalk, watercolours or natural materials. This encourages creativity, self-expression and collaboration in an expansive environment.
> 8. **Promote active exploration:** Encourage children to explore nature through nature walks, bug hunts or scavenger trails. This enhances observational skills, builds curiosity about the natural world and fosters a connection with their outdoor environment.

In Summary: Crafting a Stage for Wonder and Discovery

To summarise, the classroom is more than just a physical space; it's a vibrant stage where learning comes to life like a beautifully choreographed performance. Every corner, every resource, every thoughtful detail sets the scene for children to discover, explore and grow. Just as a theatre stage transforms with every new scene, classrooms should evolve with the needs and interests of the children, sparking curiosity and creativity at every opportunity.

Remember, the physical environment of your classrooms has a profound impact on children's social, emotional and cognitive development. It's crucial to remember that there is no single 'right' way to set up your classroom. The most effective learning environments are those that support the needs and well-being of the children. Whether your classroom is filled with neutral tones or the occasional burst of colour, the goal is to create a space where both educators and children thrive.

I loved those precious moments when I could step back and watch our classroom come alive as a bustling, interactive space where children took ownership of their own ideas. I've witnessed even the most reluctant learners find their voice, confidently collaborating, problem-solving and immersing themselves in meaningful tasks around the provision. Because they feel safe, because they know where to find things, because the classroom is theirs, they move with great purpose, independently accessing resources, making choices and shaping their own learning. Learning happens everywhere, all at once; not in a neat, linear way but in rich, multi-layered experiences driven by pure curiosity and real purpose. Those moments, when learning truly belongs to the children, are what every classroom should strive for.

The space you create holds the potential to ignite wonder. A place where children feel safe to express themselves, tackle new challenges and embark on journeys of imagination and discovery. The well-designed classroom doesn't overwhelm but instead invites children into scenes of calmness, intrigue, adventure and endless possibility. Each day becomes a new act, each crevice of the room a fresh opportunity to say, 'Wow! This is where magic happens. This is where learning comes to life!'

Key Takeaways

Designing Dynamic and Inclusive Learning Environments

- **Think of your classroom as a stage for learning:** Your classroom is the setting where learning comes alive! Look around – does every corner invite curiosity, creativity and exploration? Try stepping back and seeing it from a child's perspective. Does it spark wonder? If not, what small changes could make it more inviting? Thoughtfully defined areas, such as reading nooks, construction zones and sensory spaces, promote focused and engaging activities. Each area should support specific skills, whether that's creativity in the arts and crafts area or imaginative play in the home corner.

(Continued)

- **Balance structure with flexibility:** Children thrive in an environment with clear routines, but flexibility is key. Observe how they move through the space – do certain areas feel too crowded or underused? Be prepared to tweak layouts in response to their engagement. Try adjusting one small thing at a time and see how it impacts their play and learning. Spaces should be dynamic and evolve with children's interests and learning goals. Rotating materials and combining areas when space is limited keeps the classroom fresh and engaging without feeling overcrowded.
- **Create a space that feels calm yet engaging:** Research shows that an overstimulating environment can be as ineffective as an under-stimulating one. Look at your walls – are they bursting with displays or cluttered with too much visual noise? Try stripping some back and introducing splashes of purposeful colour instead. A feature wall, soft lighting or well-placed artwork can make all the difference. Including sensory areas with calming textures, quiet zones and elements like plants can also help create an environment where all children feel comfortable and secure.
- **Give children ownership over their learning space:** Do children know where to find things? Can they access resources without asking for help? When they take ownership of their space, they develop independence and confidence. Try involving them in setting up areas, organising materials or even deciding how displays should look. Organising materials at child-friendly levels empowers children to access resources independently and builds a sense of ownership over their learning.
- **Weave writing and maths throughout the environment:** Writing and maths should not be confined to one spot. Clipboards, writing belts, measuring tools and number lines should pop up in all areas of play. Why not try adding shopping lists in the home corner, rulers in construction or tally charts in small world play? Make writing and number work feel natural and meaningful. Providing resources like clipboards, notepads, number cards, measuring tools and writing belts throughout the setting ensures literacy and numeracy become everyday tools for exploration, problem-solving and communication.
- **Use role-play to spark language and social skills:** Role-play is a language powerhouse! Are you using it to its full potential? Try introducing props that encourage purposeful communication, like restaurant menus, doctor's forms or post office writing pads. The more real-life links, the richer the play. Role-play areas and collaborative spaces, like a home corner or construction zone, encourage teamwork, communication and empathy, helping children develop essential social skills.
- **Maximise outdoor learning:** The outdoors isn't just an extension of the classroom – it's a whole new world of learning, movement, and discovery. Think beyond taking indoor activities outside. Try setting up a mud kitchen, a nature

investigation table or an outdoor art station – complete with large canvases, easels, rollers and natural materials for mark-making on a bigger, bolder scale. The more opportunities children have to explore outside, the more confident and engaged they'll be. Adding reading areas, sensory play and open-ended resources outside encourages exploration in new and exciting ways.

- **Keep it simple:** A well-designed classroom does not need to be picture-perfect – it needs to work for you and your children. Take a step back. What feels cluttered? What feels inspiring? Try making small, intentional changes to create a space that balances beauty, practicality and meaningful learning experiences. The best classrooms grow and evolve with the children who use them! Flexibility in classroom design ensures that spaces remain engaging, functional and adaptable to children's changing needs.
- **Make the environment inclusive and representative:** Does your classroom reflect the backgrounds, cultures and experiences of all children? Try incorporating diverse books, culturally inclusive role-play props, and materials that represent different traditions. When children see themselves in the space, they feel a stronger sense of belonging and value. Thoughtfully selected materials should allow children to engage in play that reflects their own identities while promoting an understanding of different cultures and experiences.
- **Think about the flow of the space:** A classroom should support movement and collaboration. Are pathways clear? Can children transition between areas without disruption? Experiment with how resources are arranged, ensuring learning zones feel accessible. When the space works well, the learning flows more naturally. Defining purposeful learning areas, ensuring accessibility and keeping materials at child-friendly levels supports children's independence and engagement.

References

Adoniou, M. (2017) *Decoration or Distraction? The Aesthetics of Classrooms Matter, but Learning Matters More*. The Conversation. Available at: https://theconversation.com/decoration-or-distraction-the-aesthetics-of-classrooms-matter-but-learning-matters-more-83418

Barrett, P., Zhang, Y., Moffat, J. and Kobbacy, K. (2015) *The Impact of Classroom Design on Pupils' Learning: Final Results of a Holistic, Multi-level Analysis*. Salford: University of Salford.

Bottrill, G. (2018) *Can I Go and Play Now? Rethinking the Early Years*. London: Sage.

Bryce-Clegg, A. (2018) 'How to Do Outdoor Play Well', *TTS*. Available at: www.tts-group.co.uk/blog/2018/03/03/how-to-do-outdoor-play-well-by-alistair-bryce-clegg.html

Department for Education (DfE) (2024) *Early Years Foundation Stage Statutory Framework for Group and School-based Providers*. Available at: https://assets.publishing.service.gov.uk/media/65aa5e42ed27ca001327b2c7/EYFS

Department for Education (DfE) (2025) *Gross Motor Skills – Help for Early Years Providers*. Available at: https://help-for-early-years-providers.education.gov.uk/areas-of-learning/physical-development/gross-motor-skills

Early Years Coalition (2021) *Birth to 5 Matters: Non-statutory Guidance for the Early Years Foundation Stage*. London: Early Years Coalition. Available at: https://birthto5matters.org.uk/wp-content/uploads/2021/04/Birthto5Matters-download.pdf

Eslit, E.R. (2020) *Beyond Walls and Desks: Exploring the Cognitive Cosmos of Classroom Design and Its Multidimensional Impact on Learning, Creativity, and Well-being*. St. Michael's College, Iligan City.

Pemberton, L. (2022a) *Anti-Racist Leadership: Part 1 – Think Again*. Nursery World. Available at: www.nurseryworld.co.uk/content/features/anti-racist-leadership-part-1-think-again

Pemberton, L. (2022b) *Anti-Racist Leadership: Part 2 – Looking Inward*. Nursery World. Available at: www.nurseryworld.co.uk/content/features/anti-racist-leadership-part-2-looking-inward

Pemberton, L. (n.d.) *The Black Nursery Manager*. Available at: www.theblacknurserymanager.com

University of Salford (2015) *Well-designed classrooms can boost learning progress in primary school pupils by up to 16% in a single year, research reveals* [Press release]. Available at: https://news-archive.salford.ac.uk/news/articles/2015/well-designed-classrooms-can-boost-learning-progress-in-primary-school-pupils-by-up-to-16-in-a-single-year,-research-reveals.html

Voltaire (n.d.) *Writing is the Painting of the Voice*, cited in GoodReads, 2023. Available at: www.goodreads.com

Wright, S. (2016) 'Five Things to Remember about Setting up a Classroom.' *Tes*. Available at: www.tes.com/new-teachers/classroom/five-things-remember-about-setting-classroom

4
Sound Check

Unlocking Language Development

Communication is the foundation of all human connection and nurturing its development in early education is vital. Language is the powerful bridge that links us, allowing children to share their thoughts, emotions and ideas with the world. As educators, it is our privilege and responsibility to ensure that language acquisition and meaningful communication are at the heart of everything we do, providing children with the tools they need to express themselves confidently. Creating happy, language-rich environments, where adults engage in frequent, high-quality interactions with children, is essential for closing the communication gap and supporting children's language acquisition. For young learners, language development is not only vital for effective communication but also lays the foundation for academic success and social integration.

However, promoting language development can present unique challenges, especially for disadvantaged children who may face barriers such as limited access to resources and opportunities. In addressing these challenges, it's essential to recognise the concept of cultural capital, which refers to the cultural knowledge, experiences and resources that individuals bring to their learning environment. By leveraging cultural capital, educators can create inclusive and culturally responsive practices that honour the diverse linguistic backgrounds and experiences of their children.

In this chapter, we'll explore strategies for promoting language development in all children, with a particular focus on supporting those from disadvantaged backgrounds. From weaving culturally relevant materials into daily activities, to creating a vibrant, supportive classroom that celebrates and champions linguistic diversity, we'll explore exciting and innovative ways to ensure every child grows into a happy, confident communicator, ready to express themselves and connect with the world around them. As Britton reminds us, 'Reading and writing float on a sea of talk' (Britton 1970), highlighting the foundational role of oral language in literacy development.

The Power of Language in Early Years Education

Language is the key that unlocks a child's potential, shaping their learning and interactions. Just as a well-crafted script guides actors, language empowers children to express their thoughts, emotions and ideas with clarity and confidence. In the classroom, it serves as the driving force behind cognitive and social development. Educators play a pivotal role by modelling clear, precise language, enriching vocabulary and creating ample opportunities for children to practise and refine their communication skills.

This truth is echoed in national guidance, which reminds us that:

> Research shows that good interactions between adults and children make a big difference to how well communication and language skills develop. Children benefit from being with responsive and enthusiastic adults who show interest in talking with them.
>
> (Department for Education n.d.)

I wholeheartedly agree; Early Years educators are at the very core of each child's communication journey, nurturing their growth through every conversation, every new word and every meaningful interaction. In doing so, they help children grow into confident, articulate communicators – better prepared to meet the world with curiosity, connection, and courage.

Oracy, the art of speaking and listening, does more than develop communication; it empowers children to express complex ideas, fuelling both their academic success and cognitive development (Mercer et al. 2017). As J.K. Rowling's Dumbledore says in the Harry Potter film, 'Words are, in my not-so-humble opinion, our most inexhaustible source of magic' (Rowling and Kloves 2011). In our classrooms, we have the power to unleash that magic, creating spaces where language flows freely and children grow into confident, expressive communicators ready to engage with the world.

Voice 21, a leading organisation dedicated to promoting oracy education, highlights the powerful role of spoken language across the Early Years Foundation Stage. They advocate for oracy as the foundation for all learning, emphasising that strong communication skills, speaking, listening and engaging in dialogue, are essential for a child's cognitive, social and emotional development. Voice 21 inspires educators to view oracy as a vital tool that shapes confident, articulate learners who are prepared to express their ideas and interact meaningfully with others (Voice 21 2023).

Finding their Voice: Encouraging Confident Speaking and Communication in Young Learners

Language is the doorway to human connection, and before children can read or write, they must first unlock the power of their own voice. Speaking is where it all begins, whether they're sharing their excitement over a new discovery, asking thoughtful questions, or narrating their imaginative play, it's through spoken words that they start to make real sense of the world around them. A confident communicator is not just one who talks but one who speaks with purpose and clarity. From simple words to more complex expressions, language grows with every conversation, and as educators, we play an integral role in guiding children on this magnificent journey.

Research shows that when educators model rich, varied vocabulary, children naturally mirror these patterns, enhancing their language acquisition (Dockrell and Bakopoulou 2016). Daily conversations, filled with intentional language, are the fertile ground where vocabulary takes root. By revisiting words in meaningful and engaging contexts, we deepen children's understanding and make language come alive. In every moment of interaction, we offer children the chance to speak, to experiment with words and to uncover the unique rhythm of their own voice.

The Education Endowment Foundation (EEF) emphasises the intrinsic link between teaching and modelling vocabulary in the Early Years and the significant positive impact this has on children's oral language skills. This foundational practice not only enhances communication but also supports broader cognitive and academic development (Education Endowment Foundation 2018).

Practical Tips 4.1

Nurturing Language Development in Young Learners

1. **Engage with their interests:** Start conversations about what the child is currently focused on or excited about. By naturally weaving new words into the context of their interests, you're helping them build vocabulary in a way that feels relevant and engaging.
2. **Use descriptive comments:** Instead of always asking questions, narrate what the child is doing or seeing. This provides language models and reinforces their understanding without putting pressure on them to respond. When a child speaks, repeat their sentence back with added detail or corrections. This introduces more complex language without making them feel like they've made a mistake.
3. **Introduce new vocabulary in context:** Introduce unfamiliar words by connecting them to the child's current experience. This makes the language more memorable and meaningful. During activities, provide synonyms and descriptions. For example, say 'This is enormous! That means it's very, very big.' After modelling new words, ask the child to repeat them. This simple exercise helps reinforce their learning and builds confidence in using new language. Celebrate when they try to use new words, even if it's not perfect. Positive reinforcement builds their motivation and self-assurance in using language.
4. **Model clear language:** Speak slowly and enunciate. Use full sentences and introduce new vocabulary naturally. For example, during activities, describe what you're doing in detail: 'I'm cutting the red paper into squares.' Ask children open-ended questions like 'What do you think will happen next?' or 'How did that make you feel?' This encourages them to use more language to express ideas.

(Continued)

5 **Celebrate mistakes:** Allow children to experiment with language, offering corrections in a supportive way. If a child says, 'I goed to the park', respond with 'Oh, you went to the park! That sounds fun!'
6 **Dialogic reading:** When reading with children, ask open-ended questions and encourage them to predict, explain or relate to the story. This approach engages children in conversations beyond the text, building oracy skills and giving them space to share their own thoughts, feelings and interpretations.

The **STEP** approach is my simple strategy for enhancing vocabulary development in young children. This approach encourages natural language development by combining engagement, reflection and practice. It stands for:

- **S**tart: Begin by actively engaging with the child in their activity or conversation.
- **T**hink: Give them a moment to process the language you've modelled by pausing.
- **E**ncourage: Prompt the child to express their thoughts or use new vocabulary.
- **P**ractice: Reinforce the new words through repetition and continued interaction.

According to the Education Endowment Foundation (EEF), dialogic teaching, where children engage in structured, meaningful conversations, boosts vocabulary, critical thinking and confidence (Education Endowment Foundation 2019). Oracy practices also align with Vygotsky's social learning theory, which emphasises that language development is shaped by social interactions with adults and peers (Vygotsky 1978). Encouraging open dialogue, questioning and active listening fosters problem-solving and emotional regulation from a young age.

Practical Tips 4.2

Promoting Speaking Skills to Boost Language in Early Learners

1 **Plan fun vocabulary activities:** Design games or tasks that focus on introducing and repeating new words. This could be as simple as a matching game or as dynamic as a scavenger hunt for labelled objects. Set up themed talking tables based on children's interests, such as animals, transportation or seasons. Encourage children to sit together, explore objects or pictures related to the theme and engage in conversations. Adults can model rich vocabulary, introduce new words and ask open-ended questions to spark dialogue.
2 **Read aloud regularly:** Storytime is a great way to expose children to new vocabulary and different language structures. Choose books that use rich, varied

language and invite children to talk about the story. Incorporate daily storytelling, allowing children to participate. Encourage them to retell stories in their own words or create their own narratives during circle time. Use large, detailed pictures or illustrations and ask children to describe what they see. Encourage them to talk about the colours, objects and actions in the image. This helps develop descriptive language and confidence in expressing ideas, while adults can introduce new vocabulary and guide their observations.

3. **Role-play and drama:** Offering children opportunities to engage in imaginative play allows them to experiment with language, express emotions and use narrative skills. Set up themed role-play areas (e.g., a ticket office or doctor's surgery) where children can take on roles, use relevant language and explore real-world scenarios.

4. **Circle time conversations:** Structured group discussions allow children to share their thoughts while learning to listen to peers. Circle time is an ideal setting for practising turn-taking, storytelling and problem-solving. Invite children to dictate their own stories, which an adult then writes down. This practice boosts both oral language development and early writing skills.

5. **Incorporate songs and rhymes:** Songs and nursery rhymes help children remember words and sentence patterns. Use them during transitions or carpet times to reinforce language in a fun way. Research highlights that children who know eight nursery rhymes by heart at age four are among the best at spelling and reading by Year 3, underscoring the role of oral mastery in early literacy development (The Old Station Nursery 2023).

6. **Pass the mic:** In this activity, children sit in a circle and pass around a 'mic' (such as a soft toy or prop) when it's their turn to speak. The topic can be a prompt like 'What made you happy today?' or 'Tell us about your favourite animal.' Each child speaks briefly and listens while others share, practising clarity, audience awareness and active listening. This activity encourages turn-taking, confidence and respectful listening, also focus on social-emotional skills and building children's confidence to speak up in a group.

7. **Language-rich play areas:** Create specific areas in the classroom that encourage conversation – such as a puppet theatre, a construction area, or a bus role-play area, where children can interact, talk and negotiate with their peers. Adults can participate by asking questions and encouraging problem-solving dialogue.

8. **Opinion corners:** Set up different 'corners' of the classroom or hall space, each representing an answer to a fun opinion question, like 'Do you prefer winter or summer?' or 'Would you rather have a pet dragon or a pet unicorn?' Each child picks a corner based on their answer and shares their reason with the group in that corner, focusing on confidence, reasoning and turn-taking. Children practice giving reasons to support their views and responding to others' ideas in a collaborative setting, which builds confidence in speaking and audience awareness.

Tuning in: Nurturing Active Listening Skills in Young Learners

Listening is the other vital component of oracy and it plays a crucial role in how children process language, understand meaning and form their own responses. Being a good listener isn't passive; it requires active engagement. To truly listen, children need to absorb what is being said, organise their thoughts and then respond thoughtfully. This process is just as important as speaking, as it forms the foundation for the development of both reading and writing skills.

As educators, we have a responsibility to model this skill. By being attentive and responsive listeners ourselves, we show children how to tune in to conversations, process language and make connections. Active listening is key to unlocking deeper comprehension, allowing children to fully engage with language in all its forms, whether spoken, written or read. By promoting this skill, we give children the tools to not only become confident speakers but also thoughtful, reflective communicators, able to listen, understand and respond with purpose.

Both speaking and listening are intertwined, each strengthening the other and together they create the core of effective communication.

Concentration and Attention

Concentration and attention are foundational skills that support all areas of learning and development in early childhood. Young children naturally have shorter attention spans, so creating activities that are engaging, varied and age-appropriate is essential to holding their focus. Encouraging concentration can be achieved through structured routines and offering hands-on, interactive tasks that spark curiosity and motivate exploration. Activities like puzzles, small world activities and quiet story time allow children to practice sustained attention in a supportive environment. Additionally, giving clear, manageable instructions and breaking tasks into smaller steps helps young learners maintain focus, gradually strengthening their attention span. Through consistent practice and positive reinforcement, educators can strengthen children's ability to concentrate, providing a strong foundation for future learning.

Practical Tips 4.3

Cultivating Listening Skills to Engage and Inspire Early Learners

1 **Listening games:** Play classic listening games like 'Simon Says' or 'Follow the Leader'. These games require children to listen carefully to instructions and act accordingly, reinforcing the need for focused listening. You can add a twist by introducing multi-step commands to further challenge their listening abilities. Incorporate games like 'Pass the Word', where children sit in a circle and each

person adds a word to make a sentence. This game encourages listening carefully to the words before and thinking about how to respond. Another option is 'What's in the Box?', where children describe an object inside a box without showing it, and others must guess based on their description.

2. **Show and tell:** Organise regular 'Show and Tell' sessions where children bring in an object from home and talk about it in front of their peers. This not only boosts speaking confidence but also teaches them to listen actively and ask questions about what others share. Select one or two children each week to ensure everyone has a go.

3. **Sound scavenger hunt:** Take children on a sound scavenger hunt where they listen for specific sounds, such as birds chirping, doors closing or footsteps. Afterwards, gather the group to discuss what they heard. This activity heightens their awareness of sounds and helps them practice attentive listening.

4. **Echo games/call and response:** Play echo games where the adult says a word or phrase and the children repeat it back. Start with simple words and gradually move to full sentences or new vocabulary, encouraging the children to copy the correct pronunciation and rhythm of speech. Classic rhymes like *I Hear Thunder*, *The Farmer's in his Den* and *There's a Worm at the Bottom of the Garden* are perfect for encouraging rhythm, repetition and interactive listening skills in young learners.

5. **Circle time storytelling:** During circle time, tell a story and ask children to listen carefully. Pause the story at key moments and ask them to predict what might happen next or to recall details from the previous parts of the story. This encourages active listening and helps improve memory recall. Create a circle time dedicated to storytelling where children can take turns telling their own stories or sharing personal experiences. To support this, provide props or pictures to help guide their narratives. Adults can recast and expand their sentences, offering more complex language as they share. Use a story bag filled with various objects. As you tell a story, reveal the objects one by one and ask children to listen for cues in the story that relate to the objects. For example, if you pull out a small toy boat, children must listen for when the boat appears in the narrative.

6. **Sound matching games:** Use musical instruments or everyday objects to create different sounds. Let children listen carefully to each sound, then cover the object and ask them to identify which object or instrument made the sound. Or why not try an online 'Guess the Sound' video – perfect for tuning in those listening ears! After listening, ask them to identify the sounds and talk about where they might hear them in their daily lives. These activities help improve auditory discrimination and attentiveness.

7. **Partner listening or barrier games:** Partners sit facing each other with a 'barrier' between them. One child builds a simple Lego model and describes each step to their partner, who must build the same model without seeing it.

(Continued)

> Or one child draws a simple picture on a whiteboard (e.g. a house, a person, or a rainbow) and describes it step by step for their partner to copy. Then they compare! These activities promote rich language use, conversational skills, and collaborative communication – and they are fun!
>
> 8   **Be a TV broadcaster:** A fun, imaginative speaking and listening activity that encourages children to step into different presenter roles. Whether narrating a recipe, describing how a plant grows, describing the weather, or commentating over an animal video, children develop essential communication skills through playful, purposeful talk. In my experience, children absolutely love this activity. There's something magical about handing them a 'microphone' and watching them come alive with language, imagination, and confidence.

What is a Language-Rich Environment? And What Isn't it?

A language-rich environment is a setting where children are consistently exposed to and immersed in language through meaningful interactions, activities and resources. It's a space designed to encourage constant verbal engagement, where spoken words, written text and visual aids are thoughtfully integrated to support vocabulary development and communication skills. Here's what defines a language-rich environment, and what doesn't.

What is Language-Rich Development?

Frequent conversations: Educators engage with children in regular, meaningful discussions, asking open-ended questions and encouraging them to express their thoughts and ideas.

Modelling language: Adults use rich, varied vocabulary and complex sentence structures, providing children with examples to mimic and learn from.

Descriptive talk: Teachers describe actions, objects and events in detail to expand children's vocabulary and understanding of the world.

Interactive storytelling: Storytime is a regular activity where children are encouraged to discuss the story, predict outcomes and explore the language used in the narrative.

Opportunities for dialogue: Children are given ample chances to speak, ask questions and engage in conversation across the curriculum, both with adults and their peers.

Encouragement of new vocabulary: New words are introduced in context and revisited often, helping children retain and use them in their everyday speech.

Inclusive of all communication forms: Children are encouraged to express themselves through gestures, drawing or using symbols, alongside spoken and written language, acknowledging different ways of communicating.

What Isn't Language-Rich Development?

One-way communication: A language-poor environment limits dialogue, with adults mostly talking *at* children instead of *with* them. There's little opportunity for children to respond, ask questions or engage.

Limited vocabulary: Adults use the same basic vocabulary repeatedly without introducing new words or explaining more complex ideas, which limits children's language exposure. Always hold high expectations for vocabulary – children will rise to them, and often surprise you with what they can understand and use.

Silent or passive spaces: If children are expected to sit quietly with minimal interaction or if conversations are discouraged, this stifles language development.

Over-reliance on rote instruction: Environments where children are expected to repeat the same phrases or answers, with little room for exploration or creativity, fail to promote deeper language learning.

Missing opportunities for dialogue: If children aren't encouraged to ask questions, discuss topics of interest or share ideas, they miss key opportunities to develop speaking and listening skills.

Overuse of screens or passive activities: While some digital tools can support language, environments overly reliant on passive screen time without active language engagement do not contribute to language-rich learning.

Simply printing and sticking up words: It's not enough to just have words printed out and stuck up around the environment. For words to truly support language learning, they must be used in active, meaningful ways through interactions, storytelling and conversations.

Language in Play: Supporting Communication Through Interaction

In the simple yet captivating moments of imaginative play, children explore and refine their language, learning to express their ideas and feelings, listen intently and respond thoughtfully. Each playful interaction, whether in the dressing up area or discussing a favourite story character in the reading corner, becomes a lesson in conversation, where vocabulary develops organically and sentence structures steadily take shape. As educators, our role is to gently guide this process, to introduce new words and concepts that spark curiosity and to model rich, expressive language that children can echo in their own voices.

Through play, children develop far more than vocabulary. They learn how to connect with others, express their thoughts and feelings, and grow in confidence as communicators. Play provides the space for them to find their voices and learn how to share them meaningfully with the world. Play is the stage where children step into roles and try on words like costumes, exploring the world of language with curiosity and wonder. In the theatre of play, they're not merely rehearsing for life, they are living it, embodying characters, directing scenes and scripting dialogues. Through interactive play, like taking orders in a role-play restaurant or directing traffic with toy cars, children experiment with intonation, phrasing and response, strengthening their grasp of communication. Our role, like that of a director, is to set the scene with inviting props, prompts and an abundance of encouragement, allowing children to take the lead while we guide with care and intention. Here, in the different worlds that they create, language finds a home in meaningful interaction, giving them a voice in the story they're excited to tell.

Practical Tips 4.4

Building Communication Through Imaginative Play and Interaction

1. **Create role-play areas:** Set up themed spaces like a café, doctor's office or construction site with props, costumes and relevant vocabulary cards. This encourages children to take on new and exciting roles, expanding their language use naturally as they play.
2. **Use open-ended prompts:** During play, ask open-ended questions that invite children to expand their ideas. For example, 'What would you like to order?' or 'How will you fix that?' prompts them to think and respond in sentences, enhancing both vocabulary and confidence.
3. **Introduce problem-solving scenarios:** Set up a play area with resources that require active collaboration, such as building blocks to construct a stable tower, a 'broken' toy in a pretend repair shop, a bridge that needs rebuilding in small world play, a post office with parcels that need sorting and labelling or a collection of outdoor materials to build a den big enough for 3. Encourage children to work together to solve the problem, using phrases like 'What should we do next?' or 'How can we fix it?' This encourages language related to cooperation, planning and critical thinking.
4. **Introduce new words in context:** While children are engaged in play, introduce new words related to the theme. For instance, in a pretend supermarket, you might introduce terms like 'checkout', 'receipt' or 'cashier'. Repeating words in context makes them more memorable.
5. **Model expressive language:** During interactions, use expressive language and tone to convey emotions or actions, modelling how language can be used

dynamically. If children are playing as chefs, for example, you might say, 'This pasta looks absolutely delicious!' to introduce descriptive language.

6 **Encourage storytelling:** Invite children to narrate their play scenes, describing what their characters are doing or thinking. This can be done one-on-one or in small groups, helping them practise sentence structure and giving them the confidence to tell their stories in their own words.

Closing the Communication Gap for Disadvantaged Children

Recognising and embracing the cultural capital that children bring into the classroom are fundamental to creating an inclusive, linguistically rich environment where every child, regardless of their starting point, is given the opportunity to succeed. Cultural capital encompasses the unique knowledge, language and experiences children draw from their homes and communities. Every child, no matter their background, has the capacity to succeed when these unique experiences are recognised, valued, and used to support their growth.

Practical Strategies 4.5

Inclusive Early Learning to Close the Language Gap

1 **Involve parents and caregivers:** Engage families in their child's language development by providing resources and strategies they can use at home. Encourage them to read together, talk about daily activities and play simple language games. Schools can also provide access to books and materials if these are not readily available at home. Offer workshops and resources to parents that encourage home language development. Provide simple strategies like reading together, having conversations about everyday activities and singing songs and rhymes.

2 **Build on children's interests:** Tailor language activities to what children are naturally curious about. Whether it's animals, transportation or nature, talking about their interests in detail can help children engage more deeply and retain new vocabulary more effectively.

3 **Focus on small-group and one-to-one interactions:** Certain children will need greater support, best offered through smaller groups or individual interactions, where they can receive the focused attention and guidance that helps them

(Continued)

succeed. These contexts are less intimidating and allow children to practise their language skills in a supportive environment.
4. **Targeted interventions and support:** Provide additional language support for children who may need it, such as speech and language therapy or structured language programs like Talk Boost or Nuffield Early Language Intervention (NELI). These programmes are designed to give children focused support in areas such as vocabulary, sentence-building and social communication skills.
5. **High-quality conversations throughout the day:** Prioritise frequent, meaningful interactions between adults and children. Ask open-ended questions during play, introduce new vocabulary naturally and model rich language use in everyday conversations.
6. **Create a culturally responsive classroom:** Ensure the classroom reflects the cultural backgrounds of the children through books, posters and learning materials that are inclusive of different languages and traditions. Use children's home languages in activities to validate their cultural identities.
7. **Focus on oracy and listening skills:** Incorporate oracy activities, such as group discussions, storytelling, partner interviews, circle time debates and turn-taking games that encourage children to express their ideas verbally. Use the Voice 21 Oracy Framework to guide structured speaking and listening exercises.
8. **Use of visual aids and props:** Support language development with visual aids such as story props, picture cards or labelled objects around the classroom. Incorporate these into storytelling, daily routines and children's play.

For some children, limited opportunities for language and restricted access to literacy resources can pose challenges, but with the right support, such barriers need not hold them back. It is important to value each child as an individual with their own strengths and potential for growth, not through preconceived assumptions. By introducing vocabulary that relates to their lives and expanding their linguistic experiences in ways that connect with their interests and identities, we support them in finding their voice and using it with assurance. If children do not develop and learn these abilities in their earliest years, it may hinder their future success across the curriculum. According to the Department for Education's *Best Start in Life* document, 'one in four (23%) children who struggle with language at age five do not reach the expected standard in English by the end of primary school' (Department for Education 2022).

Through rich conversations, storytelling and tailored language activities, educators can create an environment that not only respects linguistic diversity but also empowers every child to grow as a confident communicator. When we foster meaningful language interactions in a setting that celebrates each child's cultural background, we create pathways for all children to flourish and develop the skills they need to succeed, bridging gaps in a supportive, inclusive way.

Supporting Bilingual or Multilingual Learners

The journey of language for a child with English as an additional language is a tapestry woven from both familiar and new sounds. Each word they hear from us in meaningful moments, while sharing a story, exploring nature or chatting over a playful activity, becomes a thread, building their confidence and fluency over time. We are not just teachers; we are language guides, modelling English with care, echoing their early attempts and gently expanding their vocabulary in ways that feel natural and inviting.

For some, this journey may begin with quiet observation, a silent period that can last months as they absorb every word, every phrase, every nuance of the language around them. Then, gradually or all at once, their voice begins to emerge – tentative at first, but full of meaning, connection, and possibility. A powerful reminder that language grows in safe spaces.

Our role is to be patient, to model language accurately and to encourage their home language alongside English. This balance enriches their understanding, honouring the full spectrum of their linguistic identity. In these nurturing spaces, children come to see that they are not choosing one language over another but embracing the beauty of both, growing as bilingual communicators ready to share their world with others.

When we encourage children to express themselves in all the languages they know, we create a learning environment that celebrates diversity and respects each child's background. Multilingualism is a powerful asset, enriching cognitive development, broadening perspectives and fostering empathy. Our role is to recognise the strengths children hold within their linguistic repertoire, using these as stepping stones to deepen their engagement, curiosity and sense of belonging. By valuing every language spoken, we're helping them understand that all voices, including their own, deserve to be heard. 'The most important message you can give parents is to keep their home language alive' (National Literacy Trust 2023).

Non-Verbal Communication

Non-verbal communication is the bridge for children who are not yet speaking, their language woven from gestures, expressions and delicate movements that reveal their inner world. For non-verbal children, each glance, wave or nod becomes a means of connection; a language of its own that invites us to listen deeply. As educators, we must tune into these cues, creating an environment where every child feels seen, understood, and truly valued. Kinderly (2021) reminds us that 'our communication must be meaningful – not just a string of instructions or descriptions'. In responding to children's silent language with intentional, resonant interactions, we're not only meeting them where they are; we're creating a space where they can develop and engage in ways that honour their unique voices.

For me, the most rewarding part of teaching has always been the magic that happens when children find their voice. Every conversation, every question and every expression of their thoughts is like watching them open a door to new possibilities. The Reception year is where this transformation happens most vividly. The shift from tentative first words to full-blown conversations, filled with excitement and curiosity, is truly remarkable. I've had the privilege of witnessing children who once spoke in simple phrases suddenly explaining their ideas, expressing emotions and engaging deeply with their peers with great gusto.

What makes this progress possible, apart from all the ideas I have listed here, is the safe, supportive culture that you create as an Early Years team. Secure relationships and a nurturing environment allow children to explore language with confidence and joy, knowing their voices are cherished and their words truly matter. For me, countless moments shine brightly: the quiet child who found the courage to share their story during circle time, the group of children lost in role-play, weaving tales together, negotiating and communicating like budding storytellers, or the spark of excitement in a child's eyes as they discover a new word and rush to use it in conversation… these moments aren't just milestones; they are some of the highlights of my teaching career.

In Summary: Setting the Stage for Confident Communicators

As we guide children on their language journey, we are both teachers and stage directors, setting the scene for their voices to emerge. Like a play unfolding, each word, gesture and heartfelt conversation builds on the last, allowing children to grow into their roles as curious communicators and confident storytellers. In our language-rich environments, we offer children a script woven with vocabulary, expression and meaning, so they can step onto life's stage ready to connect and make their unique mark on the world. It's in these magical moments, steeped in dialogue and discovery, that we witness the wonder of language unfolding, as children find their voices and offer their thoughts to the world with pure confidence and joy.

Remember, each word you share is a stepping stone for a child, guiding them to find their voice and illuminating their path towards a lifetime of connection and new discovery.

Key Takeaways
Cultivating Language and Communication Skills in Early Years

- **Create language-rich environments:** Prioritise language exposure through high-quality interactions, storytelling and a space that encourages children to speak, listen and express themselves freely.
- **Engage with children's interests:** Tailor conversations and language activities around what children are naturally curious about, making vocabulary building feel relevant and engaging.

- **Foster cultural responsiveness:** Embrace cultural capital by including materials that reflect the diverse backgrounds and languages children bring to the classroom, creating an inclusive environment that celebrates each child's identity.
- **Promote oracy skills:** Focus on speaking and listening as fundamental components of language development, helping children articulate ideas, ask questions and actively engage in dialogue at every delightful opportunity.
- **Model rich vocabulary and language structure:** Use varied vocabulary and complex sentence structures in your interactions, providing children with examples to learn from and mimic. Be ambitious: children will often astonish us with the heights they can reach.
- **Support non-verbal communication:** Recognise non-verbal cues as a form of communication, especially for non-verbal children, and respond with meaningful interactions that make every child feel valued and understood.
- **Encourage parental involvement:** Engage parents in their child's language journey by offering resources, tips and activities to support language development at home, fostering a positive home-school connection. Create and share short school videos or share leaflets with how they can support at home.
- **Provide opportunities for role-play and interactive play:** Set up themed play areas and structured activities throughout provision, allowing children to practise language skills in imaginative and varied contexts. From a bustling marketplace to an animal rescue centre or a storytelling corner, these spaces encourage children to use and expand their vocabulary, negotiate roles and engage in meaningful conversations, enhancing communication skills through playful interaction.
- **Support bilingual and multilingual learners:** Encourage children to use all the languages they know, supporting both their home language and English, to foster cognitive growth and build a bridge between cultural and linguistic identities. Integrate opportunities for the entire class to celebrate linguistic diversity, such as learning new words from different cultures or answering the register in various languages, creating a vibrant and inclusive environment for all.
- **Celebrate progress and mistakes alike:** Embrace every step of a child's language journey, from their first brave attempts to their joyful successes. Encourage them to play with words, knowing that each mistake is a stepping stone to growth. With gentle guidance and positive reinforcement, we can nurture a fearless love of learning, building confidence, curiosity and a lifelong eagerness to interact positively with others.

References

Britton, J. (1970) *Language and Learning*. London: Allen Lane.

Department for Education (DfE) (2022) *Best Start in Life: Part 1 – Setting the Scene*. Available at: www.gov.uk/government/publications/best-start-in-life-a-research-review-for-early-years/best-start-in-life-part-1-setting-the-scene

Department for Education (DfE) (n.d.) *Interactions – Help for Early Years Providers.* Available at: https://help-for-early-years-providers.education.gov.uk/areas-of-learning/communication-and-language/interactions

Dockrell, J.E. and Bakopoulou, I. (2016) 'The Role of Language in Children's Early Educational Outcomes,' *Early Child Development and Care, 186*(11), pp. 1705–1719.

Education Endowment Foundation (EEF) (2018) *Preparing for Literacy: Improving Communication, Language and Literacy in the Early Years.* London: Education Endowment Foundation.

Education Endowment Foundation (EEF) (2019) *Improving Literacy in Key Stage 1.* London: Education Endowment Foundation. Available at: https://educationendowmentfoundation.org.uk/education-evidence/early-years-toolkit/communication-and-language-approaches

Kinderly (2021) 'How to Support Non-verbal Children in Early Years'. Available at: https://kinderly.co.uk/2021/05/28/how-to-support-non-verbal-children-in-early-years/

Mercer, N., Warwick, P. and Ahmed, A. (2017) *Oracy and the Power of Talk: Improving Social and Cognitive Skills in Children.* London: Routledge.

National Literacy Trust (2023) *Understanding Multilingualism in the Early Years.* Available at: https://literacytrust.org.uk/resources/understanding-multilingualism-early-years/

Rowling, J.K. and Kloves, S. (2011) *Harry Potter and the Deathly Hallows – Part 2* (screenplay). Warner Bros.

The Old Station Nursery (2023) *The Importance of Nursery Rhymes for Children's Development.* Available at: www.theoldstationnursery.co.uk/journal/the-importance-of-nursery-rhymes-for-childrens-development/

Voice 21 (2023) *The Power of Oracy in Early Education.* London: Voice 21.

Vygotsky, L.S. (1978) *Mind in Society: The Development of Higher Psychological Processes.* Cambridge, MA: Harvard University Press.

5
Playtime Symphony

Where Learning Comes Alive

Play; those uninterrupted, instinctive moments of joy and wonder, where children freely discover and spontaneously weave together what they know with what they are yet to explore. Through play, their self-confidence radiates, spilling into their interactions, shaping their world with each newfound revelation and experience. Play is not just a pastime for children; it is their natural mode of learning and exploration. Children deserve the freedom to simply be – explorers of wonder, architects of their own worlds, unbound by constraint. It is our duty and aim to guard the Early Years Foundation Stage as a sanctuary of play and pure discovery, untainted by the weight of formality. In this chapter, we immerse ourselves in the vibrant world of play and its profound significance in early education.

Play serves as the foundation of childhood development, offering children opportunities to make sense of the world around them, express themselves creatively and develop essential skills such as problem-solving, collaboration and empathy. Delving into the significance of play, we uncover its transformative power in nurturing children's physical, cognitive and socio-emotional development. From imaginative role-playing to outdoor building activities, we'll explore the myriad of ways in which play can spark creativity, resilience and a lifelong curiosity about the world.

I've often found myself awestruck by the worlds children create when they're 'lost in play'. I recall a moment when a group of children transformed a corner of our classroom into a bustling café, complete with menus, pretend money and elaborate discussions about what 'today's special offer' should be. Without any prompting, they were negotiating roles, problem-solving when supplies ran out and practising early numeracy skills as they calculated totals and gave change.

Another time, I was invited into a hospital they had built from cushions and blankets. I became 'Doctor Underwood' (at their insistence), diagnosing invisible ailments and listening as they expertly explained treatment plans with language far beyond their years. In their world of imagination, they tackled themes like compassion, cooperation and responsibility with a depth that no structured lesson could ever achieve.

Play invites children to explore the complexities of life in a safe and joyous way. Through their laughter, their persistence and their boundless creativity, I've seen them address big questions about fairness, kindness and resilience. These are not just fleeting moments of fun; they are the building blocks of who they are becoming. It's in these priceless moments, as we step back to observe or join them in their playful worlds, that we are reminded of the profound power of play. Within play's embrace, children master the art of trial and triumph, where setbacks become stepping stones which shape their learning with courage and intent.

Let's join forces and move beyond the outdated notion that learning only happens when children are seated at desks or filling out worksheets. Senior leaders, too, must hold and champion the belief that in the Early Years, learning is vibrant, dynamic, and alive … unfolding naturally and beautifully right before our eyes – in every story acted out, every brushstroke on a canvas and every question born from imaginative chaos. These are the treasured lessons and memories that stay with them, shaping not just what they know, but who they will become.

The Science of Free Play: Why it Matters

I am deeply drawn to this beautiful definition by the National Playing Fields Association (NPFA), Children's Play Council and Playlink (2000), which portrays play as a

> dance of freedom, a child's self-directed journey, fuelled by intrinsic joy and alive with active engagement.

These seemingly simple moments of joy and exploration are far from frivolous; they are the foundation of cognitive growth and emotional resilience. As children immerse themselves in free play, their minds light up with boundless possibilities, forming neural pathways that underpin all future learning. Recent research underscores the essential role of play in children's development, clearly demonstrating how it strengthens these neural connections, enhances executive functions and builds resilience. IPA England (2023) explains:

> When children engage in play, their brains are actively forming new neural connections, strengthening existing pathways, and refining important cognitive functions.

Play is, therefore, the heartbeat of childhood, driving the growth of connections that empower children to navigate, adapt and thrive in the world. Furthermore, it makes children feel good!

Picture a child assembling an elaborate train track, carefully connecting pieces that wind through imagined landscapes filled with bridges and tunnels. To the observer, it may seem like casual fun, but beneath the surface, a complex interplay of skills is unfolding. Spatial reasoning sharpens with each curve of the track, problem-solving deepens as gaps are bridged and resilience strengthens when tracks disconnect and must be reconnected. In such moments, executive function skills, memory, focus and self-regulation are brought to life, orchestrating the intricate mental dance that shapes both intellect and character.

Free and uninterrupted play is also a rehearsal for life's social and emotional scripts. In imaginative role-play, children step into roles and navigate intricate narratives, acting as shopkeepers, doctors or explorers. They learn to juggle responsibilities, resolve conflicts and collaborate with their peers. Like actors refining their craft, they improvise, adapt to others' cues and refine their own performances. Play breaks down barriers and brings people together, creating a space where everyone belongs. It's a universal connector, crossing boundaries of age, ability and background. In play, there's no judgement, no limitations – just the pure joy of being in the moment.

Above all else, play is fun! Watch a group of children lost in play, no fixed agenda, no deadlines… just pure, unfiltered joy. It's not just their laughter that's magical; it's what's happening inside their brains. As humans, we are social creatures 'wired to play in order to learn and explore the world, relationships with others and ourselves' (Building Better Brains n.d.). During play, a symphony of chemical reactions unfolds, reinforcing joy, connection and growth. Dopamine signals to children, 'I feel good!', oxytocin deepens social bonds, endorphins elevate mood, serotonin regulates emotions, acetylcholine enhances attention and memory, and GABA (gamma-aminobutyric acid) stabilises mood. Play is a neurochemical powerhouse shaping children's development in profound ways.

Practical Strategies for Co-Opted Play

As educators, our role while children play is not to dictate but to facilitate: to create environments where play can thrive, where curiosity takes the helm and where every child feels empowered to explore, imagine and grow. A well-planned, play-rich environment is like an artist's palette, offering a spectrum of creative and open-ended possibilities. By providing quality resources, introducing open-ended materials, adding possible challenges, while also allowing uninterrupted moments of exploration, we provide the overarching tools for children to construct their own learning journeys. Each activity or resource

> should allow children some degree of choice and agency over their play: whether the playful interaction is adult- or child-initiated, play should be child-led where possible.
>
> (Hirsh-Pasek et al. 2009)

To truly unlock the power of play, we must embrace our roles as observer and collaborator. Through their play, children build trust and emotional security with the adults around them. In his extensive research on the importance of play, Dr David Whitebread states that 'playful children are securely attached emotionally to significant adults'

(Whitebread 2012). This reinforces the vital role that all educators play in championing play, not only within our Early Years classrooms but also in partnership with families. Observing a child immersed in free play offers an insightful window into their thoughts, ideas and emotions. By guiding, supporting and asking open-ended questions at just the right time, such as 'I wonder what might happen if...?' or 'Can you explain your idea?', we gently extend their thinking without overshadowing their autonomy. Our presence should be a catalyst and never a constraint, fuelling children's independence while always ensuring they feel safe and inspired to push further.

Practical Tips 5.1

Promoting Play in Your Classroom

1. **Create inviting and flexible play environments:** Design spaces that invite curiosity and creativity with open-ended materials like blocks, large boxes, tubes, guttering, art supplies and loose parts. Arrange resources so children can easily access them, fostering autonomy and encouraging meaningful exploration. Rotate resources regularly to spark renewed interest and fresh ways of playing.
2. **Integrate joy into play:** Incorporate elements of surprise and humour into play activities. For example, introduce whimsical prompts like 'Can you create a magical machine?' or 'What might live in a hidden forest cave?' to inspire rich, imaginative thinking. Add costumes and simple props to spark joy and bring their role-play ideas vividly to life.
3. **Encourage active engagement:** Provide hands-on, immersive experiences such as building challenges, sensory play stations or storytelling props. Ensure activities require movement, manipulation or decision-making to keep children deeply involved.
4. **Emphasise iteration:** Set up play scenarios that invite experimentation and refinement, such as 'design a bridge for a toy car' or 'create a new game with these rules'. Encourage children to revisit and improve their ideas, reinforcing the value of persistence and creativity. Always take inspiration from the children's passions and interests!
5. **Facilitate social play:** Design opportunities for collaboration, like group art projects, team-building challenges or role-playing games. Encourage peer interaction and problem-solving to develop social-emotional skills like empathy, communication and cooperation.
6. **Encourage critical thinking through open-ended questions and challenges:** Use open-ended questions to prompt exploration and deeper thinking, such as 'What could you try differently?' or 'What happens if you do this?' Observe how children engage with their environment to understand their thought processes before stepping in. Introduce occasional challenges, either at the start of the day

or when adding new enhancements, to spark curiosity. For example, add unique resources to each area, like natural items in the sand tray or real tins and boxes in the home corner, to inspire fresh ideas and iterative learning.

7 **Celebrate process over product:** Shift the focus from outcomes to experiences. Praise effort, curiosity and problem-solving during play rather than the finished creation. For example, highlight how a child in the home corner explored different roles, collaborated with peers and came up with creative scenarios for their pretend play, rather than focusing on the finished 'meal' they prepared.

8 **Dedicate time for play:** For deep learning to take root, children need ample, unhurried time to explore, revisit and extend their play. Ensure daily schedules include uninterrupted playtimes, free from rigid expectations. Prioritise extended periods of child-led play where children can immerse themselves deeply in their activities without feeling rushed. Balance structured learning with open-ended exploration to encourage creativity and engagement. Communicate the value of play to parents and caregivers at every opportunity, emphasising its role in cognitive, social and emotional development.

When intentional design meets a heartfelt respect for children's autonomy, play transforms into a vibrant space where creativity and joy flourish.

Continuous Provision

Step into an EYFS classroom and you will hear it … the quiet hum of discovery alongside the joyful buzz of independent learning. Continuous provision is the ever-present invitation, whispered from shelf and tabletop: 'Come, create, discover, grow.' Continuous provision offers a landscape of possibility where children move freely, explore deeply and learn instinctively. It is the dependable backdrop of resources that children revisit and repurpose as their ideas grow. Here, they engage independently – practising, refining, and embedding their learning through self-directed exploration. Mastery is not a moment but a journey, one that unfolds through repeated experiences, joyful experimentation and uninterrupted immersion in the magic of play. Indoors and out, every provision area whirrs with the quiet energy of purpose. Blocks balanced into sky-high towers, role-play scenes spun into intricate narratives, number lines explored with eager fingers or feet. Choice is at their fingertips, raising autonomy, encouraging perseverance and nurturing the deep, intrinsic motivation that turns play so seamlessly into powerful learning.

Continuous provision is the invisible thread that ties together child, adult and environment. The teacher, ever the watchful co-constructor and guide, shapes the space with intent, ensuring that each resource offers challenge, sparks a myriad of questions and provides endless opportunities for curiosity-driven learning. The right balance must be struck; familiarity that builds confidence, interwoven with new provocations to stretch young minds further. High-quality, purposeful resources stand ready to be transformed by imagination, while the environment whispers quiet encouragement: 'Try again, explore, discover more.' When continuous provision is carefully crafted and intentionally enhanced, children do not wait for learning to be handed to them; they seize it, mould it and make it their own. They become active and deeply absorbed, building knowledge alongside the habits of self-regulation, curiosity and resilience that will carry them far beyond the Reception year.

Practical Tips 5.2

Maximising the Impact of Continuous Provision

1. **High-quality, inspiring resources:** Every item within your continuous provision must earn its place. Resources should be carefully chosen to ignite curiosity, encourage deep thinking and support meaningful play. Open-ended materials, such as blocks, natural objects, real-world items, invite limitless possibilities, while rich texts, mathematical manipulatives and creative tools should be engaging, accessible and developmentally appropriate. These materials must be well-maintained and appealing, ensuring they remain a source of wonder rather than becoming overlooked clutter.

2. **An environment that invites and provokes:** Your learning space should be a seamless blend of familiarity and intrigue; a landscape of security that invites risk-taking, experimentation and bold ideas. Thoughtfully arranged provision areas, with clear pathways and purposeful zones, allow children to navigate freely and independently. Displays should celebrate children's thinking and ideas, reinforcing that their contributions shape the space around them. Outdoor areas should mirror the depth of learning opportunities found inside, offering space to move, build, dig, create and explore in a way that complements indoor learning.

3. **Well thought out provision areas:** Each area of provision must have a clear and deliberate purpose, supporting learning across all areas of development. Whether it's a cosy book nook that invites storytelling, a maths area rich with real-life problem-solving opportunities, or a small-world space that sparks narrative play, each zone should be well-resourced and ready to inspire. Spaces should evolve thoughtfully, responding to children's needs and interests while maintaining a consistent structure that provides security and confidence. However, it's important to remember that the purpose we assign to an area as adults may pale in comparison to the adventures, meanings and discoveries a child uncovers there. Their imagination stretches far beyond the intended, often redefining spaces in ways we might never predict. Think outside the box at times; ask, observe, listen and tune into what your cohort loves to do. They may see purpose in so much more than what is immediately obvious and by embracing their perspectives, we unlock even richer opportunities.

4. **A deep understanding of continuous provision:** Effective continuous provision is not about filling a space with a variety of resources and hoping for the best, nor is it about dictating exactly how every area 'should' be used (although some rules and routines are essential). It requires intentional design, where the environment and materials are carefully considered yet remain open-ended enough to invite creativity and personal interpretation. Teachers act as skilled observers, facilitators and enhancers of learning, tuning into how children interact with the space, recognising when to step in and when to step back and knowing how to introduce new provocations without overwhelming. Continuous provision is an approach, a philosophy – one that puts learning in children's hands.
5. **The power of revisiting and refining:** Children learn best when they can return to their work, refine their ideas and build upon previous experiences. A well-structured environment allows them to pick up where they left off, whether that's continuing a construction masterpiece, developing a story they started last week or revisiting a challenge that once felt too tricky. Consistency in resources and space allows learning to build. Changes should be intentional, supporting progression rather than causing disruption. Mastery is built up over time, through repetition and sustained engagement. Continuous provision, alongside a broad and ambitious curriculum, provides the perfect framework for this.

Outdoor Play

The outdoors, with its rich textures, sights and sounds, becomes an unmatched canvas for creativity and discovery. Nature offers infinite materials that children can transform into anything their minds can envision. From building dens under the canopy of trees to stirring imaginary soups in a mud kitchen, outdoor play connects children to their environment and nurtures their innate sense of wonder. Seasonal changes provide endless opportunities for exploration: collecting fallen leaves in autumn, observing blooming flowers in spring or summer scavenger hunts that turn the natural world into an adventure. I recall one sunny afternoon, a group of children ventured outdoors, declaring themselves 'explorers on a treasure hunt'. They turned leaves into maps, pebbles into treasures and their imaginations transformed the space into an uncharted island. As I watched, I was reminded of the limitless creativity that play inspires and how outdoor settings amplify the magic of discovery and wonder.

Do remember, outdoor play is *not* about transferring indoor activities to an outside setting; it is a wholly different experience. The uniqueness of the outdoors, with its unpredictable elements and natural resources, creates dynamic learning opportunities that cannot be replicated indoors. The diverse textures of bark and stones, the movement of wind and water and the wide open spaces encourage active, sensory-rich experiences. This environment supports children in developing determination, spatial awareness and physical agility.

Outdoor play is vital for physical development and gross motor skills. Activities like running, climbing and balancing engage large muscle groups, promoting strength and coordination. Whether constructing ramps, navigating obstacle courses or simply exploring the terrain, children can improve their physical coordination and thinking skills in equal measure. The freedom to move, experiment and explore without the confines of walls allows children to experience joy and a profound connection to the outdoors.

Margaret McMillan is often credited with the saying, 'The best classroom and the richest cupboard is roofed only by the sky,' reflecting her emphasis on the value of outdoor learning environments (McMillan 1919).

Practical Tips 5.3

Unlocking the Power of Outdoor Play

1. **Embrace all weathers:** 'There's no such thing as bad weather': Equip children with the right clothing, like waterproofs and wellies (ask parents to support this), to explore the outdoors in all seasons. Rainy days can mean puddle jumping, while snowy days inspire building snow creatures. Encourage exploration of the environment regardless of the weather to cultivate resilience and a deep appreciation for the natural world.
2. **Make use of free resources:** Incorporate everyday items such as tyres, cardboard boxes and large wooden planks into outdoor play. These can become climbing frames, balance beams or tools for fort building. Consider reaching out to parents or local businesses for donations – you'll be surprised how many people are happy to contribute materials that can spark children's creativity and sense of adventure.
3. **Harness the power of nature:** Encourage children to interact with natural materials like leaves, sticks, stones, seeds, bulbs, pebbles and flowers. Create mud kitchens, build fairy houses or paint with natural pigments. Nature offers endless opportunities to inspire creativity and sensory exploration.
4. **Provide easy access to play materials:** Set up accessible outdoor storage, like crates or shelving, where children can independently choose materials for their play. Provide sheets, string and natural materials like sticks and leaves for children to construct their own hideouts. Rotating or adding to outdoor resources regularly ensures variety and keeps children engaged. Easy access empowers children to take the lead in their play.
5. **Prioritise space and movement:** Designate areas for different types of play, such as running games, climbing activities or quiet spaces for reflection. Provide open-ended opportunities for movement, ensuring the space supports both energetic and mindful activities.

6. **Encourage choice and variety:** Offer a diverse range of activities, from gardening and sensory paths to active games and simple outdoor role-playing setups. Provide opportunities for group challenges, such as building a shared structure or creating a large piece of art with natural materials. Cater to different interests and developmental needs, giving children the freedom to express themselves, take risks and develop a broad range of skills.
7. **Get messy and hands-on:** Incorporate mud kitchens, water play and sensory trays outdoors to encourage free tactile exploration. Set up an area with old pots, spoons and soil to let children engage in messy, imaginative play. Let children dig, pour, splash and create without fear of mess. These experiences support fine motor skills, creativity and emotional expression.
8. **Experience the living world:** Create opportunities to observe and interact with living things. Plant seeds, care for a garden or take time to marvel at the tiny creatures that flutter, crawl, and buzz through the outdoor world. Offer items like rocks, pinecones and driftwood to spark open-ended exploration and creativity. Organise activities based on the time of year, such as leaf rubbings in autumn or a bug hunt in summer. Encourage children to collect treasures, like feathers or interesting stones, to use in later crafts or storytelling. These activities build a connection to the environment and encourage curiosity about the natural world.

Outdoor play is a world of its own, full of energy and joy. It gives children space to think big, take risks and connect deeply with the natural world. The rustle of leaves, the grip of climbing branches, the thrill of a race across an open space – these are the moments that grow confidence and awaken the spirit of adventure.

In Summary: Play – the Heart of Learning and Growth

In these final thoughts, childhood emerges as a stage where play takes centre spotlight, offering a vibrant space where young minds rehearse for the complexities of life. It is through this rehearsal that resilience, the cornerstone of success, is nurtured in the small but powerful acts of persistence born from play. When a train derails or a painted masterpiece doesn't turn out as planned, children must rewrite their scripts, problem-solve and try again. It is in this messy beauty of play that they learn life's most enduring lesson: setbacks are not the final curtain call but an invitation to rise and create anew. Play becomes their rehearsal for a future brimming with possibilities – a stage where they develop their sense of self, build confidence in their abilities, and practise the characteristics of effective learning: playing and exploring, active learning and thinking critically.

Our role as facilitators of play is to ignite curiosity, offering children the time, space, and freedom to explore and create. Let's say no to rigidity and celebrate the magic that happens when children are free to play.

> ## Key Takeaways
>
> ### The Transformative Power of Play in Early Childhood Development
>
> - **Play as emotional exploration:** Play offers children a safe space to explore complex emotions, whether through role-playing, storytelling or problem-solving. This emotional rehearsal helps children build empathy and self-awareness, preparing them to navigate real-life challenges with greater confidence.
> - **Play builds lifelong resilience:** Through trial and error during play, children learn to embrace setbacks as opportunities to think critically and try again. These moments of persistence form the foundation of resilience; a skill that extends far beyond the classroom.
> - **The power of autonomy in play:** Child-led play nurtures independence. As they make choices, direct their explorations and follow their instincts, they develop a deep sense of ownership over their learning, shaping their world with every decision they make.
> - **Play as a driver of intrinsic motivation:** Play taps into children's intrinsic motivation by rewarding curiosity and creativity with joy and accomplishment. This internal drive reinforces their engagement and willingness to explore without the need for external incentives.
> - **Unstructured play inspires innovation:** Unlike guided activities, unstructured play allows children to invent, iterate and discover solutions to self-created challenges. This open-ended approach encourages innovative thinking and prepares children for complex problem-solving in the future.
> - **Outdoor play encourages risk-taking:** The natural unpredictability of outdoor play environments encourages calculated risk-taking, such as climbing, balancing or navigating obstacles. These experiences build courage, promote decision-making skills and help children to assess and progress their own capabilities.
> - **Play shapes executive function:** Activities like organising a picnic in the role-play area, following a multi-step recipe in the mud kitchen, or taking turns in a game of 'what's the time, Mr Wolf?' strengthens executive function skills, including memory, focus and self-regulation. These are vital tools children carry with them, both in learning and in life.
> - **Play connects children to their environment:** Interacting with natural materials like sand, water, pinecones, tree bark and feathers during outdoor play deepens children's connection to the environment. This builds a sense of wonder and responsibility towards the natural world, encouraging sustainable behaviours

such as caring for plants and wildlife, reusing and repurposing materials, and understanding the impact of their actions on the environment.
- **The role of reflection in play:** When children pause to revisit their play, retracing their steps, questioning their choices, and making sense of their discoveries, they unlock deeper learning. A simple prompt like, 'What did you figure out?' or 'How would you do it differently next time?' transforms play into a moment of growth. Reflection strengthens resilience, teaching children that every challenge is a stepping stone, every mistake a lesson, and every attempt a chance to refine, rebuild and rise.
- **Play as a celebration of diversity:** Play unites children of different abilities, backgrounds and perspectives, creating a space where inclusivity and understanding naturally flourish. Through shared experiences, children learn the value of collaboration and respect for peer differences, building a more empathetic community for all.

References

Building Better Brains (n.d.) *How Play Rewires the Brain*. Available at: https://buildingbetterbrains.com.au

Fisher, J. (2020) *The Place of Play in Key Stage 1 Classes*. Greater Manchester Combined Authority. Available at: www.greatermanchester-ca.gov.uk/media/4108/the-place-of-play-in-ks1-julie-fisher.pdf

Hirsh-Pasek, K., Golinkoff, R.M., Berk, L.E. and Singer, D. (2009) *A Mandate for Playful Learning in Preschool: Presenting the Evidence*. New York: Oxford University Press.

IPA England (2023) *The Science of Play: How Play Impacts Brain Development*. Available at: https://ipaengland.org

McMillan, M. (1919) *The Nursery School*. London: J.M. Dent and Sons.

National Playing Fields Association (NPFA), Children's Play Council, and Playlink (2000) *Best Play: What Play Provision Should Do for Children*. London: National Playing Fields Association.

Whitebread, D. (2012) *The Importance of Play: A Report on the Value of Children's Play with a Series of Policy Recommendations*. Toy Industries of Europe. Available at: www.toyindustries.eu/resource/the-importance-of-play-report/

6
Directing the Journey

Planning, Performing and Reflecting

In early childhood education, a profound truth unites us all: the foundations we lay today shape the futures of tomorrow; a great privilege and an even greater responsibility.

The EYFS Framework serves as the rich, fertile soil that underpins Early Learning, providing the guidance, structure and standards necessary for effective practice. Children arrive in your setting, already growing and developing like a unique 'seedling'. They rely on this consistent 'soil' teamed with the expertise of skilled practitioners, to truly thrive. The framework expects that the essential conditions for growth are in place, offering the structure and consistency needed to support children's continued development. It is the culture and whole Early Years team, the gardeners if you like, who create the positive environment, tending to each plant with intentionality, nurturing its unique potential and providing the experiences, skills and values needed to help it bloom in a setting conducive to effective learning.

The bespoke curriculum that you design for your children is paramount: the carefully chosen blend of experiences and opportunities that enrich children's development over the year. Just as gardeners select the right mix of nutrients, sunlight and water based on each seedling's needs, Early Years teams must design and deliver a curriculum that aligns with the EYFS Framework while meeting the individual needs of the children in their care. The framework creates the ideal conditions for the curriculum to 'take root', ensuring children can develop in a supportive environment, at their own pace. The learning and development, assessment, and safeguarding and welfare requirements are the essential layers of this rich soil. When curriculum design, framework expectations and setting culture intertwine, the result is a prosperous environment where every child can grow in their own unique way.

In this chapter, we will delve into our part as instigators and guides. We'll discuss how we create a setting that nurtures growth, how we might shape provision and design a curriculum that is broad, flexible and awe-inspiring. Our outlook and flexibility are integral to this process; we must be willing to adapt on a daily basis, knowing when to change approaches that haven't worked so well and knowing when to step back and marvel at how far children have come. We'll reflect on how we assess, support and challenge them appropriately, stepping in with purpose to subtly move their learning forward without hindering their natural curiosity.

This chapter is in three sections. Section 6.1 explores the EYFS as an overarching framework. Section 6.2 is an overview of each of the areas of Learning and Development with some practical ideas to consider for your setting. Section 6.3, Planning your pedagogy, is about the educator's role in action; how we bring learning to life in everything we do.

I will share my reflections and notions on how these principles might 'blossom' in your classroom, accompanied by a wealth of practical ideas and approaches across the seven curriculum areas that you can explore and adapt with your team, to enrich your everyday practice.

6.1

The EYFS Framework

At first glance, the EYFS Framework may seem daunting; a comprehensive document filled with terms, requirements and expectations. But it is important to remember that it is not a rigid set of rules to follow verbatim. Instead, it is a guide designed to support educators in creating environments where children can truly succeed. It sets out clear goals and statutory requirements that must be adhered to, but how you meet them, the curriculum you design and the teaching approaches you adopt, is where your expertise, creativity and understanding of your unique cohort and context come into play.

The EYFS Framework, to me, is like the stage on which every child's unique story begins to unfold. It sets the foundation for lifelong learning, equipping children with the skills, knowledge and attitudes they need to step confidently into the spotlight as they transition into Key Stage 1 … and beyond. The framework truly champions early childhood education, recognising just how important and transformative these Early Years are for every child.

At the heart of it all are the children; the stars of the show! The EYFS Framework reminds us to tune into their passions, strengths and challenges, to observe and listen with awe and to craft learning experiences that are meaningful and relevant to them. And like a great production, it's built on relationships, those backstage collaborations with parents, colleagues and the wider community. These bonds, the trust and connections we build, are the invisible threads that hold the entire performance together, giving children the confidence and security to step into their role and shine.

One of the most important messages in the EYFS Framework is that it's not a tick-list. It explicitly discourages using developmental milestones as rigid checkboxes. Instead, it values meaningful observations that inform our professional judgement and help us meet children where they are. As the *Development Matters* guidance states, 'Assessment should not be about lots of data and evidence' (Department for Education 2023). Practitioners should draw on their knowledge of each child and trust their own professional judgement to respond sensitively, plan purposefully and nurture each child's unique path of progress. Our focus should be on truly knowing the child, not simply recording every achievement.

I value how the framework emphasises the balance between nurturing care and purposeful learning, ensuring children are not only kept safe and healthy but are also well prepared for the next steps on their educational journey.

What the EYFS Seeks to Provide

- **Quality and consistency in all Early Years settings, so that every child makes good progress and no child gets left behind.** Every child has the right to experience a secure, enriching environment tailored to their needs, where their progress is celebrated and their needs are addressed. It's about creating spaces where no child feels invisible and every step of progress, no matter how small, is acknowledged and rejoiced.
- **A secure foundation through planning for the learning and development of each individual child and assessing and reviewing what they have learned regularly.** I believe a secure foundation is built on knowing each child deeply; understanding their interests, challenges and unique ways of learning. Through thoughtful planning, responsive and adaptive teaching and ongoing, non-intrusive assessments, Early Years teams can ensure that each child's roots are strengthened, allowing their learning to grow in every direction.
- **Partnership working between practitioners and with parents and/or carers.** Partnerships with families are integral to the success of an Early Years setting. By building this essential alliance, listening actively and valuing parents and carers as the first educators, we create a trusting community that truly supports children's development and champions the Early Years. A successful home–school partnership is all about working together, building trust and creating a shared journey supporting each child's growth, learning and happiness.
- **Equality of opportunity and anti-discriminatory practice, ensuring that every child is included and supported.** This is the heart of our work: ensuring *every* child feels valued, respected and seen for who they truly are. It's about challenging barriers and addressing biases face on.

'When we give every child the best start in their early years, we give them what they need today. We also set them up with every chance of success tomorrow' (Department for Education 2023).

Overarching Principles of the EYFS

The Early Years Foundation Stage (EYFS) is guided by four overarching principles.

Understanding the Unique Child

The EYFS principle of the unique child reflects the profound truth that every child is an individual with their own story waiting to unfold. Throughout my humbling career, I've seen first-hand how nurturing this individuality can completely transform the way children engage, learn and develop over this crucial year.

Honouring each child's individuality throughout the Reception year means banishing a one-size-fits-all approach and taking the precious time to truly understand their strengths and needs. This involves creating environments rich in opportunities for open-ended exploration, where every child can find their own way to engage meaningfully. It means stepping back, observing, listening carefully and using what we witness to adapt the planning and provision; whether offering materials that reflect a child's interests, incorporating their ideas into new activities or giving them the space and support they need to develop at their own pace.

By focusing on the unique child, I've seen how small, thoughtful adjustments can help children feel understood, valued and capable. It's about supporting their development at every step of the way, celebrating their individuality and creating the conditions where every child feels they belong and can progress in their own special way.

What You Might See

1 **Engaged, curious children:** Proactive children actively exploring their environment, making personal choices about what interests them and immersing themselves in play and discovery. You'll see them problem-solving, creating and experimenting with a range of quality resources, whether it's building a water run with pipes, role-playing in the home corner or investigating natural materials outdoors. They will be on the move, engrossed in their learning and above all they will be happy and animated. How wonderful!
2 **Intentional, adaptable environments:** A well-organised space designed to encourage exploration and independence. You'll notice a mix of familiar favourites and new resources tailored to the children's interests and needs, with both indoor and outdoor areas offering diverse opportunities for all learners. Classroom displays will reflect the children's work, celebrating their achievements and creating a sense of belonging for the cohort as a team.
3 **Responsive practitioners:** Practitioners observing, listening and interacting purposefully with children. They'll be on the move, sometimes kneeling on the floor to join a child's play, or at other times stepping back to allow independence. Their interactions will be natural, supportive, guiding and extending learning without interrupting children's natural flow.

What You Might Hear

1 **Children's voices filled with wonder and curiosity:** Lively and engaging conversations as children share ideas, ask questions and explain their thinking to others: 'Look what I've made!' or 'Come and see this!' You'll hear laughter, problem-solving discussions and delegation and the occasional squeal of delight when something exciting happens (from adults and children).
2 **Practitioners supporting and extending learning:** Practitioners encouraging children through open-ended questions and positive reinforcement: 'Tell me more about that', 'What do you think might happen next?' or 'You're working so hard – what else could you try?' With warmth and intention, their words will help children grow in confidence and explore ideas more deeply.

3   **A balanced rhythm of calm and energy:** The hum of a busy, dynamic space where children are free to explore, balanced with moments of quiet focus and reflection. You might hear the calm concentration of children threading beads or a lively sing-along echoing from the carpet area.

Positive Relationships in Action

We explored this theme in Chapter 2. The relationships we build with children are crucial. Positive relationships are rooted in trust, consistency and genuine care. These relationships form the secure base from which children feel confident to explore, learn and develop. In my practice, I've found that being fully present with children, taking the time to listen to their thoughts and feelings and responding with empathy and intrigue are essential steps in cultivating these heartwarming connections.

Building trust begins with small, intentional actions. I've used calm, predictable routines to create a sense of security and adjusted my interactions to meet each child's emotional needs; whether through offering comfort during moments of anxiety, providing encouragement to take on new tasks or challenges, or sharing joyful, unhurried moments of play. I love marking each achievement, however small, as a way to build their sense of belonging and self-worth.

These relationships shape both individual development and also the dynamics of the group. By modelling kindness, patience and compassion, I've seen how children begin to form positive relationships with one another, creating a community where they feel safe, respected and valued. Positive relationships are the foundation for a child's confidence and ability to thrive within a supportive and connected environment.

What You Might See

1   **Warm, nurturing interactions between practitioners and children:** Staff actively engaging with children, making eye contact and responding to their needs with care and attentiveness. Practitioners who are mentally present – attuned to the children's actions and activities and actively listening with genuine intrigue to a child as they describe an event. You might see staff offering comfort to a child who's upset, celebrating a small achievement with a high-five or gently encouraging a child to join in with a group activity. These small, consistent actions create a secure and trusting environment.
2   **Children forming meaningful relationships with their peers:** Children collaborating during play, sharing resources and helping one another. For example, a child might patiently explain how to play a simple throwing and aiming game outside or invite a peer to join their role-play game in the cafe. These moments of kindness and teamwork reflect the positive relationships modelled by practitioners.
3   **A sense of belonging and inclusion:** Displays featuring children's work, family photos and community connections to celebrate diversity and

individuality. You'll see children confidently navigating their space, knowing they are valued and that their voices are heard. The group feels like a small community where everyone has a place.

What You Might Hear

1. **Encouraging and supportive practitioner language:** Phrases like 'I'm here if you need help', 'You're doing such a great job' or 'How do you feel about trying that again?' Practitioners using positive reinforcement, gentle encouragement and open-ended questions to build confidence and independence.
2. **Children's voices sharing and connecting:** Lively conversations as children share their ideas, solve problems together or comfort one another. You might hear, 'Do you want to be the shopkeeper?' or 'I can help you carry that!' These interactions reflect the kindness and empathy modelled by practitioners.
3. **Moments of joy and collaboration:** The hum of a happy, engaged group, with bursts of laughter and exclamations of pride. A child might shout, 'Look what we made together!' while others cheer them on. You might also witness persistence unfolding right before your very eyes as a child reflects and finds their way forward.

Enabling Environments

An enabling environment is safe, subtly stimulating and supportive to its core. It's where all children are given equal opportunities to succeed alongside motivating adults who are responsive to children's individual needs. Such an environment effortlessly cultivates children's curiosity at every opportunity and encourages each individual to immerse themselves in a play-based, awe-inspiring curriculum that empowers them to dive into new challenges and build upon their prior learning at their own pace.

When I think of an enabling environment, I picture happy and resilient children, I hear purposeful talk and I notice children developing by the minute due to the positive and nurturing culture that has been carefully created by all major stakeholders. The room is filled with endless possibilities that children can access freely and that span the whole Early Years curriculum. Resources are thoughtfully chosen to include what children know and what they've yet to explore. Adults naturally deliver timely, quality interventions that lead to invaluable 'eureka' moments.

An enabling environment also advocates equality and inclusion naturally and consistently, giving children the many opportunities to learn about and appreciate diverse needs, cultures, religions and backgrounds. A space where every child feels recognised and respected, regardless of their differences.

An enabling environment consists of an Early Years team that know their children inside out and who interact with each induvial child with utmost dedication and enthusiasm. In summary, enabling environments are the whole package; the kit and caboodle – be that the people, the setting, the community, the indoor and outdoor areas, the culture created and of course; happy, safe and motivated children.

What You Might See

1 **Children deeply engaged in activities:** Some might be role-playing in a home corner, while others are building structures, painting or exploring the outdoor area, all reflecting their individual interests and developmental stages. Practitioners crouching down to the children's level, observing their play, asking open-ended questions or modelling language and behaviours.
2 **Parents actively engaged:** Parents are valued, key partners in their child's journey, sharing their skills or stories, engaging in purposeful conversations with staff and contributing valuable feedback and support that shapes the learning environment and enhances each child's experience.
3 **A welcoming, inclusive space:** Thoughtfully arranged areas for play, quiet moments and focused activities, with meaningful visual displays featuring children's work, photos and input from families, creating a strong sense of community. A space equipped with high-quality, age-appropriate resources that are well-maintained, offering both challenge and support to inspire exploration and development.

What You Might Hear

1 **Meaningful interactions between children and staff:** Practitioners engaged in purposeful conversations with the children, taking the time to listen closely, respond to their ideas, celebrating success and thoughtfully supporting their learning journey at a pace that is right for them.
2 **Children's voices and joy:** Confident children sharing ideas, negotiating and expressing themselves freely, unafraid to take risks and who are fully immersed in the delight and wonder of their surroundings.
3 **Staff dialogue and collaboration:** Practitioners engaging in reflective conversations, sharing observations and collaboratively planning to ensure the environment and learning opportunities meet the ever-evolving needs and interests of the children.

Learning and Development

Children develop and learn at different rates and understanding this variability is key to meeting their unique needs. Some race ahead in certain areas, while others take their time to find their stride. Recognising this individuality is essential in creating Early Years practices that support all children effectively. I've taught children who could write their names beautifully on day one of Reception and others who needed time to build their confidence before picking up a pencil. I've had children who jump straight into a range of social situations, forming friendships with ease and others who prefer to quietly observe until they feel ready to join in. These differences are what make our job so rewarding because every child's progress is their own story and we get to help write the next chapter.

The Characteristics of Effective Teaching and Learning outlined in the framework (paragraph 1.18) guide practitioners in creating environments where children can explore, think critically and become active participants in their own learning journey. By tailoring experiences to align with each child's interests, strengths and developmental stage, Early Years teams enable children to progress in a way that feels natural and empowering. For me, it's about meeting every child where they are, not where a chart or milestone says they should be. Celebrate the journey, not the finish line: when we keep this mantra at the heart of everything we do, we shift from racing ahead to noticing every bend, pause and moment of wonder along the way.

The framework's commitment to inclusion ensures that the education and care of all children are supported, including those with special educational needs and disabilities (SEND). By embedding practices that value diversity and equity, practitioners can create learning opportunities that are accessible and meaningful for every child. This involves adapting teaching approaches, providing appropriate resources and working closely with families and specialists to meet each child's unique needs.

What You Might See

1 **Children engaged in individualised learning experiences:** Children exploring a variety of activities that align with their interests and developmental stages. You might see one child engrossed in a construction project, another carefully threading beads to build fine motor skills and a third quietly observing a water play activity before joining in when they feel ready. A small group of children may be with a staff member in the reading area joining in with a story; fully engaged and focused. Every child is immersed in meaningful experiences across the provision that reflect their unique needs.
2 **Inclusive practices supporting all learners:** Adaptations seamlessly embedded into the environment to support children with special educational needs and disabilities (SEND). For example, sensory-friendly areas for children who need a calm space, visual timetables to support understanding of routines or alternative tools like pencil grips or communication lanyards – all designed to support every child to access learning in a way that works for them.
3 **A well-organised and inviting environment:** You'll see a thoughtfully designed space that encourages independence and exploration, with clearly defined areas for different types of play and learning. Open shelves with accessible resources that invite children to make their own choices. Both indoor and outdoor spaces are used to their fullest potential, offering diverse opportunities for physical activity, creativity and quiet reflection.

What You Might Hear

1 **Children expressing themselves with confidence:** Children talking about their discoveries and sharing their thinking: 'I'm making a bridge for the cars!' or

'This water goes faster when I pour it here!' For some children, their voices will reflect curiosity, excitement and confidence as they explore and test ideas. For others, they will be actively engaged in activities that interest them alongside staff members who are supporting their next steps.

2 **Practitioners using encouraging and inclusive language:** You'll hear members of staff adapting their language and tone to suit individual children, ensuring everyone feels supported and understood. Practitioners will be able to speak confidently and naturally about each child, drawing on deep knowledge of where they are on their learning journey. They will be championing the children at every opportunity and will know exactly what their next steps are. You will hear the Early Years team members discussing the children's progress at key intervals throughout the day. This collaborative approach ensures that all staff share the bigger picture when it comes to their cohort and that slowly but very surely, gaps are being closed on a daily basis.

3 **Collaborative problem-solving and reflection:** Children reflecting on their learning and working through challenges together: 'Let's try this way instead' or 'What if we add more blocks?' You might also hear practitioners gently guiding this process: 'What happened when we tried that? What else could we do?' This collaborative approach helps children develop critical thinking and persistence.

Creating Your Curriculum

The curriculum consists of everything you want children to experience, learn and be able to do (Department for Education 2023): a blueprint for wonder, discovery and growth.

Your curriculum should be rooted in the statutory Early Years Foundation Stage Framework, offering a secure base from which to build across the seven areas of learning. But the real magic lies in how you bring it to life, through your creativity, expertise and the unique needs of your children. By designing a curriculum that reflects your setting, your children and your team's collective values, you create an environment bursting with opportunities. Through rich experiences, purposeful play and joyful teaching, you spark curiosity and set the stage for every child to flourish. What an exciting privilege that is!

Your curriculum should be deeply rooted in the present, highly responsive to the 'moment', while always keeping an eye on what's just around the corner for each child. It must be broad, balanced and highly ambitious, capturing the full range of children's capabilities and talents. Make it rich with experiences, engaging in its delivery and inspiring in its intent. Ensure every child, regardless of their starting point, has access to learning that excites and challenges them to progress. Be intentional in closing the gaps for some but ensure to ignite a spark in all.

Your curriculum must go beyond simply acquiring knowledge. It should weave in the development of skills, behaviours and attitudes that will prepare children for future learning and help them navigate the world with confidence and care. It's about crafting rich, ambitious and holistic experiences that will enable all children in your care to progress. What makes your setting unique? How does it reflect the lives, culture and context of the children and families you serve? How can you ensure their learning builds sequentially, helping them connect the dots and deepen their understanding?

So many questions; the challenge is knowing where to start.

It's about capturing the spirit of your children, weaving in your EYFS values, and embracing your community, all while ensuring learning is rich, purposeful and full of possibility. Here's some ideas to guide you in crafting a curriculum that truly inspires.

Step 1: Your Vision and Values

Before diving into the intricate details, take a big step back and truly reflect on the bigger picture.

- What do you want children to experience, learn and remember from their time with you?
- What makes your setting unique?
- What values underpin everything you do? (e.g., curiosity, creativity, independence, resilience)
- How does your setting reflect the community, culture and backgrounds of your children?

This is your chance to establish the heart of your curriculum. It should feel authentic, purposeful and inspiring.

Step 2: Use the EYFS Framework as Your Foundation

Your curriculum must be firmly rooted in the statutory EYFS Framework.

- Familiarise yourself with the seven areas of learning and how they interconnect.
- Recognise that the Characteristics of Effective Teaching and Learning shape how children engage with and retain knowledge.
- Consider how your curriculum ensures progression, helping children know more, do more, and remember more over time.

Think of the framework as the structure that holds everything together. Your curriculum is how you bring it to life in your setting. Please note here: 'The Early Learning Goals (ELGs) should not be used as a curriculum or in any way to limit the wide variety of rich experiences that are crucial to child development' (Department for Education 2025).

Step 3: Know Your Children

An effective curriculum must meet the needs of your cohort: never a generic, one-size-fits-all approach.

- Observe and reflect: What are your children's interests, strengths and key focus areas?
- Identify starting points: Where are they now? What do they need to develop next?
- Consider cultural capital: What experiences will enrich and inspire them?
- Your curriculum should be flexible, allowing space for children's natural curiosity to shape the learning journey.

Step 4: Map Out Progression and Learning Intentions

Now it's time to plan the journey. How will children build upon their skills and knowledge throughout their time with you?

- Set high expectations for all. Ensure your curriculum is highly ambitious, inclusive and designed with the intention that every child will succeed.
- Plan for sequential learning – how will knowledge and skills progress over time?
- Ensure a balance of direct teaching, provision-based learning and child-led experiences so that children can wonder, explore and build knowledge in ways that are both guided and joyfully discovered.

Your curriculum should be a living, breathing story – fluid and ever-evolving, shaped by the children it serves and the progress they make.

Step 5: Meaningful Learning Experiences

- Now, bring your curriculum to life through rich, engaging experiences.
- How will you introduce learning in a way that captivates and excites?
- What purposeful play opportunities will help embed new knowledge and skills?
- How will you weave in real-life experiences, stories and outdoor learning?

Your provision should be dynamic and responsive, adapting to children's interests while ensuring core learning is embedded through everyday experiences.

Step 6: Assessment and Impact

Assessment should be meaningful, not excessive. It's about knowing children well and supporting their development.

- Use observation as your primary tool: watch, listen and interact.
- Track progress without turning learning into a data-driven exercise.
- Reflect on impact: Are children engaged? Are they making progress? What adjustments are needed?

Assessment should inform your teaching, not dominate it. Keep it focused and purposeful.

Step 7: Review, Reflect and Adapt

A great curriculum grows with your setting. It evolves, improves and responds to the needs of your children.

- Regularly review: What's working? What needs tweaking?
- Gather insights from children, parents, and your team to refine your approach.
- Stay inspired – draw from research, best practices and the world around you.
- Your curriculum is never 'finished'; it's a living, breathing document, constantly shaped by the children you teach.

So, start with your vision, build with intent and bring it to life with joy. Fundamentally, your curriculum should be 'alive'. It must cover the seven areas of learning in equal proportion and be ever evolving, deeply rooted in the needs of all children and just as inspiring for you as it is for them. Let's dive into the seven areas now.

6.2
The Areas of Learning and Development

The seven areas of learning in the EYFS provide the framework upon which you shape and build your curriculum. Here is an overview of each area with some practical ideas to consider for your setting.

Personal, Social and Emotional Development: Building their Inner Compass

'Children's personal, social and emotional development (PSED) is crucial for children to lead healthy and happy lives and is fundamental to their cognitive development' (EYFS Framework 2024). It's where children begin to understand their place in the world and how to connect with those around them. Without this foundation, no other learning can truly 'stick'. When children feel safe, secure, valued and heard, they form bonds, take risks, embrace challenges and communicate their needs and ideas with confidence, knowing they are supported every step of the way. When children feel safe, valued and heard … they excel.

Educators must aim to create a culture where these qualities naturally take root, supporting children to develop a strong sense of self and a belief that they are capable, worthy and always valued. Just as crucially, it's about supporting them in managing their emotions, giving them the tools to self-regulate, cope with daily challenges and form thoughtful, positive relationships with those around them.

When shaping your Personal, Social and Emotional Development (PSED) curriculum, consider your vision: creating a culture where children feel safe, valued and empowered every single day. PSED underpins everything we do in Early Years. Fundamentally, it involves helping children understand themselves, manage feelings, and build positive relationships.

Practical Tips 6.2.1

Nurturing Personal, Social and Emotional Development in Reception

1. **PSED is in everything we do:** Personal, Social and Emotional Development cannot be covered in a lesson – it's embedded in every single interaction, every consistent routine and every choice we make. Whether we're modelling turn-taking, narrating emotions or guiding children through problem-solving challenges, we are constantly shaping how they see themselves and relate to others.
2. **Relationships first, always:** Strong, trusting relationships are the foundation of all learning. Children need to know they are valued. I make it top priority to truly know my children inside out, to take note of their interests, their fears, their quirks, so that they feel safe enough to explore, take risks, and develop confidence in who they are.
3. **Think about progression over the year:** Reception is the opening chapter of a child's journey into greater resilience and independence. Here they begin to steady their emotions, face conflict with support, give shape to feelings through their words and actions, and learn to stand a little taller in themselves. Begin where they are in September and, step by step, nurture greater resilience, self-awareness and self-management as the year unfolds. With gentle support, help them to follow routines with confidence, make wise and healthy choices, dress and organise themselves, and keep going when tasks feel hard. With patient guidance and repeated practice, fragile first attempts give way to surer steps, until confidence and self-belief take root.
4. **Provide a secure environment for risk-taking:** For children to try, fail and try again, they need to build their resilience and feel secure. Ensure your setting has predictable routines, repeated opportunities, clear expectations and a culture where mistakes are seen as valued learning opportunities. This allows children to take emotional risks, like sharing a new idea or asking for help.
5. **Small steps are big wins:** It's easy to focus on the big milestones, but PSED thrives in the tiny moments. The first time a child confidently asks to join a game, the first time they say, 'Can I have a turn after you?' Celebrate these small steps because they are the foundation for lifelong confidence and social success.
6. **Give children the words they need:** Language plays a huge role in emotional development. Embed emotional literacy into everyday interactions, modelling how to express feelings and needs. Giving children the words to communicate their emotions empowers them to express themselves constructively.
7. **Encourage independence, but offer scaffolding:** Self-regulation, turn-taking and conflict resolution don't develop overnight. Never expect children to manage their emotions from the outset; scaffold the process. Practice strategies together, role-play scenarios and gradually step back as they build confidence in handling situations with greater independence.

> 8. **Balance structured and free-flow opportunities:** PSED is strengthened through real-life experiences. Create intentional moments within play, outdoor exploration and everyday interactions where children can test social skills, manage emotions and practice self-regulation in a natural setting. For example, setting up a café role-play, inviting children to build an obstacle course together, or creating shared artwork all offer opportunities to practise turn-taking, manage emotions and build positive relationships.
> 9. **Model and narrate emotional responses:** Children learn how to manage emotions by watching us and others around them. I always make a point to model self-regulation: 'I feel a little frustrated right now, so I'm going to take a deep breath before I respond.' This kind of open narration helps children internalise strategies for handling their own feelings.
> 10. **Create a culture of kindness and inclusion:** PSED is about belonging. Your classroom should be a place where every child feels safe, valued and celebrated for who they are. This means intentional representation in books and resources, active discussions about differences and fairness and daily moments of warmth and connection.

PSED isn't something we deliver – it's something we live, in every glance and gesture. Every smile, every reassuring word, every opportunity to listen and connect shapes how children feel about themselves and their place in the world. And that, for me, is the most important thing we do.

Physical Development: Where Movement Meets Mastery

Physical development is the gateway to purposeful movement and growing autonomy. It's not simply about letting off steam; it's about the joy of movement and the confidence it brings. The way children interact with the physical world shapes their learning in every area. Through movement, they discover their capabilities, push their boundaries and learn to trust their bodies. Fine motor skills – the gentle grip of a pencil, the delicate threading of a bead, become the building blocks for creativity and communication while gross motor skills – the exhilaration of climbing, balancing, jumping or spinning, give them the freedom to explore their world with growing assertion.

There's something magical about a child discovering what they are capable of. The pride in their eyes when they master a skill, no matter how small, is priceless. It's a reminder that physical development promotes self-determination and physical confidence. As educators, we have the privilege of cheering them on in these moments, knowing that every shift in balance or burst of effort is a step towards a stronger, more capable version of themselves.

When planning for physical development, it's not just about providing movement opportunities – it's about creating a curriculum that helps them feel capable in their bodies and secure in their efforts. It begins with the basics in September and deepens steadily, offering more challenge and possibility by July.

Practical Tips 6.2.2

Embracing the Joy of Physical Development

1. **Think beyond the obvious:** Physical development isn't just about running, climbing or throwing. It's also about balance, coordination, core strength, flexibility and control, all of which support other areas of learning. Consider a mix of activities that promote different physical skills, from yoga and dance to obstacle courses and den-building.

2. **Build in progression:** Make sure activities grow in challenge and complexity over time. A child who starts the year learning to jump confidently might be leaping between platforms by summer. Those early pencil grips become detailed drawings. True progress happens when children feel safe to challenge themselves, step by step, in their own time.

3. **Maximise the outdoor space:** The outdoor area is a treasure trove for physical development, but it needs thought. Ensure there's a variety of opportunities available; spaces to run, climb, balance, dig and build. Ensure the seasons don't slow the pace – weather-proof options keep movement alive all year round.

4. **Fine motor all year round:** It's easy to focus on gross motor play, but fine motor skills need consistent opportunities too. Plan daily activities to strengthen small muscles – playdough modelling, threading beads, using tweezers, scooping, squeezing sponges, turning keys in locks and finger gym stations – all of which help prepare children for writing when they're ready.

5. **Offer real-world physical challenges:** Physical development should support independence in daily life. Include activities that mirror real-world tasks – learning to button a coat, zip up a bag, pour from a jug or carry a tray carefully. These activities build confidence and self-reliance.

6. **Encourage risk-taking (within reason!):** Children need safe opportunities to take risks; balancing on logs, climbing higher than before, jumping that little bit further. Design spaces and activities that encourage calculated risk, helping them learn to trust their bodies and build resilience.

7. **Think about left-handed learners:** It's something I always consider when setting up activities. Are scissors available for left-handers? Are seating arrangements thought through so they don't bump elbows? Small adaptations make a huge difference in ensuring every child can develop their skills comfortably.

8. **Make movement part of learning, not an extra:** Physical development shouldn't be separate from the rest of the curriculum – it should weave through everything. Bring movement into phonics (skywriting letters), maths (hopping to count) and storytelling (acting out actions). Moving helps learning stick!

9. **Incorporate music and rhythm:** Dance, rhythm games and music-based movement are powerful for developing coordination, balance and timing. Whether it's clapping rhythms, action songs or full-body movement sessions, these activities develop control and are just pure joy!
10. **Celebrate every milestone:** Physical development is filled with personal victories. Whether it's a first time on a balance bike, managing a tricky zip, or climbing to the top of the outdoor climbing frame, acknowledge and celebrate those golden moments. Every step forward and every moment of progress whispers, 'You can.'

When planning for physical development, I don't just think about what's happening now – I think about what's next. I want children to feel strong, capable and in control of their own bodies, with the confidence to take on the world, one movement at a time.

Communication and Language: The Power of Connection

Communication and language are the fine threads that weave a child's world together. It is through language that children express their needs, share their precious thoughts and make sense of their world. Every question they pose and every heartfelt story they tell is a declaration of their desire to make meaningful connections. Communication and language open doors to all other learning across the curriculum. It is how children build relationships, explore new ideas, convey their sense of wonder and begin to shape their own unique narrative.

For me, the magic of communication lies in those moments when a child finds their voice, when they move from a hesitant murmur to an animated storyteller. A teacher's encouragement and intuitive guidance is paramount. We are the ones who scaffold their language journey, offering the right words at the right time, modelling curiosity and creating the safe spaces where children feel free to express themselves. Language is about empowerment; giving children the tools to express who they are and what they dream of becoming. As educators, our role is to nurture this growth and listen deeply. When we value their words, we show them that their voice matters and that is a lesson that will carry them far beyond the Early Years.

Practical Tips 6.2.3

Unlocking the Power of Communication and Language

1. **Build a language-rich environment:** A child's language journey is shaped by what they hear around them. Fill the setting with words – stories, songs, conversations, labels, displays and meaningful print. Children should be immersed in language at every opportunity.
2. **Progression matters:** Some children enter with limited vocabulary, while others are already holding conversation with ease. Plan with progression in mind,

(Continued)

stretching and supporting all learners. Consider what their language journey will look like over the year. How will you broaden their vocabulary and ability to articulate their own ideas? How will you close the gaps for those with limited vocabulary and do so at the right time and pace?

3. **The power of open-ended questions:** Stop and think about the questions being asked. Instead of closed questions like *'What colour is this?'*, use prompts that invite deeper thinking and conversation, such as *'Why do you think that happened?'* or *'What do you notice about…?'* Children need space to explore their thoughts aloud.

4. **Conversations over interrogations:** Language develops through genuine conversations, not through adults firing questions in a scatter gun approach. Listen as much as you speak and let children's words guide each interaction. Focus on back-and-forth exchanges where their ideas are valued and encouraged.

5. **Storytelling is everything:** Stories aren't just for story time – they should be woven into every part of the school day. Storytelling develops imagination, vocabulary and sequencing skills, as well as introducing the past and new concepts. Use puppets, small-world play, or co-create tales together. Make storytelling a natural and exciting daily occurrence.

6. **Create opportunities for talk, everywhere:** Talk does not belong only on the carpet! Oh no! It happens in the mud kitchen, in construction, while waiting for lunch. Set up provocations that spark discussion – an unusual object to explore, or a problem to solve together. Children should never be without opportunities to express themselves through talk.

7. **Model, model, model!:** Children learn language from the people around them. Constantly model rich vocabulary, sentence structures and curiosity. If a child says *'big truck'*, expand, *'Yes! A huge, powerful truck with enormous wheels!'*. Let children hear language at its richest, and watch it take root. Children are hungry for language… never doubt their ability to understand and use ambitious vocabulary.

8. **Celebrate all forms of communication:** Not every child is confident in speaking straight away, and that is okay. Tune in to non-verbal cues, gestures and body language too. Some children communicate best through drawing, role-play or movement before they find their words. Valuing all communication builds confidence.

9. **Give them the words for feelings:** Language is a powerful tool for understanding emotions. Model emotional vocabulary so children can articulate how they feel. Instead of *'Are you sad?'*, say, *'You seem frustrated. Would you like to talk about it?'* Helping children name their emotions empowers them to express their needs.

> 10 **Listen like it's the most important thing in the world:** Because it is. When children see that their words matter and that adults genuinely listen, they learn that their voice is powerful. Slow down, make eye contact and show that what they say has great value. This, more than anything, gives children the confidence to use their voice. Always be *present* when a child is talking, even though there are 101 other things to think about.

Literacy: Unlocking the World of Words

Literacy is a bridge to infinite possibilities! Yes, it includes teaching them to read and write. But it's so much more. It's about empowering children to explore, imagine and express themselves. Through stories, they step into worlds beyond their own, discovering characters who spark empathy and grand ideas that ignite curiosity. Writing gives them the means to turn fleeting ideas into something lasting and real.

Literacy is a profound tool of transformation. It's a true gift and the way we present it defines its impact. A teacher's role is pivotal in making literacy an adventure, not a set of chores. Stories that are thoughtfully chosen, questions that stir curiosity, and encouragement given in those tentative first attempts at writing become moments that ripple far beyond the classroom. With our passion and guidance, we instil the belief that their words have power and we inspire them to see reading and writing as daily adventures, rich with magic and meaning.

The EYFS Framework highlights the importance of supporting children's literacy development from the very start, ensuring that every child has the tools they need to explore, express and connect. As the National Literacy Trust notes, 'Literacy is essential. Without literacy, it's hard to live the life you want. From your earliest years, literacy skills help you develop and communicate. But when you have a tough start in life, it's easy to fall behind' (National Literacy Trust, n.d.). This underscores the responsibility we have as educators to create environments rich in language, stories and opportunities for children to develop their voices and discover the power of words.

When planned thoughtfully, literacy unfolds like an adventure, where books open new worlds, writing becomes an act of self-expression and every child begins to see themselves as a reader and a writer. We must bring words to life giving the children the confidence to communicate and tell their stories with pride.

Of course, phonics is an essential tool in teaching children to read and write but it's not the 'beating heart' of literacy. We know we need to give fidelity to a systematic phonics scheme that provides structure, consistency and a clear pathway for decoding. But let's be clear: this is not where the magic of literacy is found!

A true passion for reading and writing is born from stories that captivate, characters that enchant, the joy of thoughts set free on paper, and the wonder of language that allows ideas to take flight.

Practical Tips 6.2.4

Developing a Love for Literacy Through Play and Exploration

1. **Build a curriculum that grows with them:** From early mark-making to writing full sentences, plan opportunities for children to move forward at their own pace, ensuring that each step feels exciting, not overwhelming. Literacy progression must build confidence at every stage.

2. **Books, books and more books:** A book-rich environment is a MUST. Stories should be everywhere, in every area of provision, not just the reading corner. Whether it's a cookbook in the role-play kitchen, a nature book by the mud kitchen or poetry by the painting station, literacy should weave into their world seamlessly. Tell stories often – they light the way for language to grow.

3. **Create a love for writing, not just the mechanics:** Yes, phonics is important, but literacy is so much more than phonics sessions. Writing isn't just about letter formation. Provide real reasons to write – letters to fairies, treasure maps, recipe cards, postcards home, invitations to tea parties, instructions for magical potions and signs for their own imaginary worlds.

4. **Talking comes before writing:** If they can't say it, they'll struggle to write it. Build in lots of discussion, drama and role-play before children put pen to paper. Oral storytelling, puppet shows and retelling stories in their own words help children to build the confidence they need to turn their ideas into marks on a page.

5. **The magic of seeing writing in play:** There's something magical about a child writing in play – a shopping list in the home corner, a label for their junk-model rocket, a 'wanted' poster for a missing teddy. These 'goosebump' moments are solid gold because they show children see writing as a meaningful tool to convey their ideas. Encourage this by providing rich opportunities to write: signs for dens and doorways, postcards from enchanted lands, treasure maps, spell recipes, shopping lists, party invitations and secret notes tucked into tiny envelopes.

6. **Keep it hands-on and multi-sensory:** Plan messy, playful, sensory literacy experiences. Writing in sand, tracing letters with paintbrushes, making marks with twigs in mud. The more ways children can explore letter formation, the more embedded their learning becomes.

7. **Give them the time and space to write freely:** Some children will write fluently by the summer term, others will still be finding their way. Don't rush the process or put pressure on them too soon. A love of writing takes root in its own time – when children are ready, they will bloom.

8. **Foster a passion for words:** Language is beautiful and we all want children to fall in love with words! Introduce them to new, exciting vocabulary, celebrating the way words sound, feel and create pictures in our mind's eye. The more words they know, the richer their reading and writing will become.

> 9 **Celebrate every success, big or small:** Whether it's their first scribble, their first recognisable word or a full sentence, celebrate it all! Building confidence is key, and when children feel like authors, they become excited to keep going. Always acknowledge the effort, not just the finished piece.
> 10 **Make literacy an adventure:** Above all, literacy should be exciting. Bring in authors, turn books into immersive experiences, let children create their own stories to share. A love for reading and writing comes from the magic we create around words and texts.

Seeing children become readers and writers is one of the greatest privileges of our job. Let them write! Let them read! Fill their world with words and watch their confidence soar. Encourage a passion for reading and writing at every opportunity. When they see and feel your enthusiasm, when they hear you marvel at a beautiful sentence or get lost in the rhythm of a story ... they'll feel it too. Passion is infectious and when children sense that reading and writing are exciting, meaningful and theirs to own, they'll step boldly into the adventure right beside you.

Mathematics: Building a Sense of Order and Discovery

Mathematics in the Early Years is a world of discovery – solving puzzles, exploring quantities, reasoning and making connections. While structured maths teaching plays its part, the most profound mathematical moments emerge through play; counting out picnic plates in the home corner, building towers that test balance and height or pouring water to explore volume and measure. By immersing children in rich, hands-on experiences, modelling curiosity and nurturing a positive attitude, we lay the foundations for deep mathematical understanding, where numbers, shape, space and measures become part of their world.

For me, maths is about captivating a sense of wonder. A well-planned learning environment provides the perfect context for mathematical conversations, where adults can embed learning, challenge children's thinking and introduce rich vocabulary at every possible opportunity. Through these interactions, we cultivate a space where children feel confident to engage with mathematical ideas and see them as tools for understanding their world.

Children should have frequent opportunities to count confidently and develop a deep understanding of numbers to 10, exploring their relationships and the patterns within them. By incorporating varied resources, such as tens frames, small pebbles, or other manipulatives, we enable children to build and apply this understanding in meaningful ways. This secure base of knowledge and vocabulary is essential for mastering the foundations of mathematics.

Equally important is offering rich opportunities for children to develop spatial reasoning skills across all areas of mathematics, including shape, space and measures. These experiences not only deepen their understanding but also empower them to see the connections between mathematical concepts. Encouraging children to spot number patterns, recognise shapes, make comparisons and take risks builds strong mathematical habits and a positive, problem-solving mindset. When they are encouraged to talk about what they notice and engage in playful mathematical exploration, they realise that maths isn't just about answers – it's about noticing and wondering. As educators, we guide children to discover the wonder in maths, showing them how it weaves through our world, supporting them to face each mathematical challenge with joy and courage. Maths in the Early Years is about exploring, questioning and discovering – it's about helping children see that numbers and patterns are woven into everyday life. No to tick lists and ploughing through worksheets. Yes to deep, flexible mathematical knowledge, rooted in children's starting points and carried forward in joy.

Practical Tips 6.2.5
Creating a Rich and Engaging Mathematical Journey

1. **Maths is everywhere – make it visible:** Maths does not only happen at a table. It's in every corner of your setting. Allow children to see maths in action, whether it's counting snack pieces, comparing shoe sizes, spotting patterns in nature or estimating how many jumps it takes to cross the playground. The more we bring maths into real, everyday experiences, the more naturally it becomes part of their thinking and play.

2. **Know what to teach and when:** And no, it's not a case of cramming everything in. Take the time to layer learning carefully, starting with strong number sense before moving onto more abstract concepts. Build in space for children to master and revisit early number concepts, rather than pushing forward too quickly. It's better for a child to be truly secure with numbers to 10 than to be pushed on to number bonds they don't yet understand.

3. **Build on natural connections and interests:** The best maths moments often happen organically through play. Tune into children's passions and interests. If they're building ramps in the outdoor area, explore angles and speed; if they're setting up a shop, play with money. Don't shoehorn maths into play – notice where it lives naturally and build from there.

4. **Hands-on first, always:** Children need to see, feel and manipulate maths before they can work with it abstractly. Model the use of concrete resources such as counters, cubes, pebbles, tens frames, number lines and natural materials before expecting them to understand anything on paper. Maths is something to be actively explored, not merely written down.

5. **Focus on problem-solving, not just answers:** If children are simply given answers, they're not actually thinking mathematically. Make sure they are solving

real-life problems, spotting patterns and explaining their reasoning to others. The goal is to embed maths in contexts that truly matter to children.

6 **Model mathematical thinking out loud:** Voice mathematical thinking in everyday moments:

- '*I wonder if we have enough cups for everyone at snack time?*'
- '*Hmm … this tower keeps falling over. What could we do to make it stronger?*'
- '*I think I need two more steps to reach the other side. What do you think?*'

Children absorb mathematical thinking when they see it modelled in playful ways.

7 **Keep it joyful! Build excitement around maths:** Weave in games, songs, storytelling, movement, music and playful challenges. A shape scavenger hunt, a dice-rolling race, or a rhythmical counting game can turn learning into delight. Add drama and imagination – pretend to be number detectives solving mysteries, builders measuring out blocks, or shopkeepers working with coins. Use outdoor spaces to hunt for patterns in leaves, count bird calls, or measure giant strides across the playground. Bring in rhythm and rhyme, clapping patterns and chanting number sequences with joy. When maths is playful, physical and woven into stories and adventures, children come to live and breathe it as naturally as play itself.

8 **Be flexible – follow their lead:** Some days, they're eager to count everything in sight; other days, they want to pour water and explore volume. Teaching needs to bend with their curiosity. Rigid plans falter when they fail to meet children where they are. The art lies in following their lead and their curiosities, noticing what captures their attention and allowing maths to grow from those moments.

9 **Small steps lead to big success:** Early maths is a journey. Rushing children through concepts before they're ready doesn't serve them well. Focus on deep understanding, not quick wins. Seeing a child confidently explain why 5 is made up of 2 and 3 is far more valuable than having them simply recite number facts with no real meaning.

10 **Celebrate their mathematical thinking:** Not only right answers but the process – the reasoning, the problem-solving, the persistence. When a child notices a pattern, tests an idea, or discovers a new way to solve a problem, acknowledge it. '*I love how you spotted that pattern!*' or '*That was such a clever way to figure that out!*' Moments like this make maths matter.

If we get maths right in the Early Years, children don't just *do* maths, they live and breathe it, through their play and everyday interactions. And that is the true foundation for lifelong mathematical thinking.

Understanding the World: Cultivating a Spirit of Exploration

Understanding the world involves guiding children as they uncover the wonders of their surroundings – the people they meet, the places they go, and the natural world unfolding around them. Every question they ask and every discovery they make ignites their critical thinking skills and cultivates a deep appreciation for the diversity of life.

For me, it's where children begin to see how their own lives connect to a broader story, both past and present. As educators, we are their guides on this journey of discovery, showing children how to look deeper and wonder more: grounding that curiosity in a sense of belonging, helping children feel rooted in their own story while introducing them to the vastness of what lies beyond.

One of the most profound aspects of this learning is helping children develop a sense of chronology. At this age, children often see the world egocentrically, with themselves at the centre. We must build on what they recall, gently introducing the concept of sequence, helping them understand that the past has an order. Through stories, timelines, and shared discussions, we can help children piece together how events connect, building a foundation for historical thinking and their sense of place in time.

The natural world invites children to notice and respond. A melting ice cube might hold their gaze. The shimmer of frost can prompt a quiet question. These fleeting encounters are anything but small – they ignite curiosity. Scientific thinking begins not with a worksheet but in muddy hands and wondering eyes. It is strengthened by experience and deepened over time. When we pause with them and value their observations, we show them that asking why is powerful.

I believe that teaching children to understand their world is about creating a sense of awe and wonder. Whether it's exploring the natural environment around them or fully appreciating different cultures, our role is to ignite that spark of curiosity and ensure it burns brightly.

Practical Tips 6.2.6

Bringing Understanding the World to Life in Reception

1. **Start with their world and build outwards:** Young children naturally focus on what's familiar. Always start by helping them explore their own family, traditions, community and surroundings before gradually widening their view to different places, people and experiences. Their sense of belonging comes first, making it easier for them to connect to the bigger picture.
2. **Keep it relevant and meaningful:** Children engage best when they can relate learning to their own lives. Make sure to link new ideas to their daily experiences; weather discussions after a rainy walk, historical discussions inspired by their grandparents' stories or exploring different foods that connect to their home life. When learning feels personal, it sticks.
3. **Bring the past to life through storytelling:** Young children don't naturally grasp the concept of time in the way adults do. Instead of dates and facts, introduce history through stories, objects and experiences – looking at photographs, using

role-play or reading books that transport them to the familiar past. The more we make it tangible, the more they begin to understand the idea of 'before now'.

4. **Give them hands-on science and discovery:** Scientific thinking at this age is all about exploration and experimentation. Provide sensory-rich experiences, whether it's watching ice melt or dissecting a flower. It's about encouraging their 'what if?' thinking, rather than simply giving them the answers.

5. **Make the most of your local area:** Understanding the world starts on their doorstep. Use local visits, maps, landmarks and community members to help children connect with where they live. A simple walk to the market or a chat with a local firefighter brings learning to life in ways that books and screens never could.

6. **Use cultural capital to expand their world:** Every child comes to school with a unique set of experiences. Some may have travelled widely, others may never have been beyond their town. Make sure that all children have rich, diverse experiences within your setting, whether that's learning about local festivals, tasting foods from different countries or exploring traditional dances and music. These moments help children see beyond their own experience and feel connected to the wider world.

7. **Ensure your environment reflects the world around them:** From globes and maps to artefacts and books, I make sure my classroom is filled with resources that help spark conversations about the wider world. What's in their role-play area? Their book corner? Their small-world setup? If we want children to be curious about different cultures and communities, they need to see them every day in their environment.

8. **Encourage exploration and questions:** The best learning comes from children's own questions. Never shut down a 'why?' or a 'how?' Instead, turn it back to them: 'What do you think?' 'How could we find out?' Model curiosity, showing them that learning is an ongoing journey rather than something with a set response.

9. **Make time for awe and wonder:** There is something magical about watching a child marvel at a rainbow or stare in wonder at the stars. Pause in these moments, building in space for questions and deep conversation. Sometimes, the most powerful learning isn't planned ... it's caught in the moment.

10. **Connect everything back to their own story:** At the heart of Understanding the World is helping children find their place. Make sure every experience and discussion helps them see how they belong. Whether it's exploring their own family history or understanding the passing seasons, it's all about helping them feel rooted, connected and curious about what comes next.

Understanding the World is the catalyst for deeper thinking and broader horizons. When we bring the past to life, explore the present with excitement and open doors to the wider world, we spark a lifelong love of learning. Because the more children understand their world, the more confident they become in shaping their place within it. And the most magical part? We learn new things too – every single day.

Expressive Arts and Design: Nurturing Creativity and Innovation

Expressive Arts and Design is joy in its purest form; it's where children paint their thoughts, dance their feelings and build the worlds that exist in their imaginations. It involves giving children the space and time to create without boundaries. We must provide them with the tools and opportunities to experiment, discover, take risks and convey their emotions in ways that words cannot always capture. It is in these special moments of uninhibited creativity that children reveal the colours of their personality.

This area of learning is vast and vibrant. For me, there is nothing more inspiring than witnessing a child lose themselves in a creative moment, whether through music, drama, role-play or the simple joy of turning a blank page into something beautiful. Experimenting with music, singing, movement, storytelling, drama, role-play, painting, sculpting and using materials in inventive ways can lead to magical outcomes. Our role is to offer inspiration and to honour their unique interpretations of life around them. Through our infectious enthusiasm and unwavering belief in their capabilities, children discover that creativity isn't given, it's already theirs.

Practical Tips 6.2.7

Cultivating Creativity in Expressive Arts and Design

1. **Build a culture that values creativity:** Creativity flourishes in environments where it is celebrated and encouraged. Create a space where every idea is valued, where there's no fear of 'getting it wrong' and where children see that expressing themselves is just as important as any other area of learning. If you're excited by their ideas, they'll feel that excitement too.
2. **Make art and design accessible every single day:** Creativity should be woven throughout the day. Ensure there are permanent creative spaces where children can independently access resources, whether that's a well-stocked art station, a role-play area bursting with props or an inviting space for music and movement.
3. **Provide a broad and balanced range of creative experiences:** Offer a wide range of progressive experiences each term, such as sculpting with clay, large-scale collaborative artwork, shadow play, junk modelling, digital art, body percussion, dance improvisation, creative design challenges and more. The more varied the opportunities, the more chance children have to find their own creative voice.
4. **Plan for progression, not just experiences:** Creativity develops over time. Think carefully about how skills evolve, how children move from making marks

to forming shapes, from exploring sound to composing their own rhythms, from dressing up to constructing full narratives in their role-play. Creativity deepens when children are given time and encouragement to refine their ideas.

5 **The process matters more than the product:** As a team, remember that the journey is more important than the outcome. Focus on the joy of creating, not the pursuit of perfection. A child smearing paint with their hands, layering paper to make 'something unknown', or playing the same three drum beats over and over is immersed in learning and that's what matters most. Yes, there are times when we model new skills, maybe teaching them to print with different objects or modelling how to hold a triangle when tapping a beat, but the true connections are made when children figure out these things for themselves.

6 **Use the environment to inspire:** The classroom itself should invite creativity. Use display boards as 'living galleries', showcasing children's evolving work rather than just finished pieces. Provide open-ended resources, like fabrics, natural materials and unusual objects, that spark ideas rather than dictate any fixed outcomes. Inspiration is everywhere. Sometimes, all it takes is rearranging a space to ignite new possibilities.

7 **Invite experts, artists and musicians into the setting:** There is something magical about children seeing creativity in action. Inviting local artists, dancers, designers, musicians or storytellers into the setting provides a huge burst of inspiration and helps children see that creativity is valued beyond the classroom. I once invited a local artist into my class, and the awe on the children's faces was unforgettable – curiosity sparked and their eagerness to create was unstoppable.

8 **Think about cultural capital and representation:** Creativity should be a window into the wider world. Consciously plan experiences that reflect different cultures, traditions and artistic styles, helping children see the beauty in diverse forms of expression. Whether it's learning a traditional African dance, painting in the style of Kandinsky or listening to folk music from around the world as they come in on a morning, exposure to different creative influences is so, so powerful.

9 **Give children time to 'get lost' in their creations:** Creativity can't be rushed. Ensure children have uninterrupted moments where they can deeply engage in creative experiences, whether that's casting spells in a puppet theatre, designing enchanted lands from scrap materials, creating soundscapes with unusual instruments, or transforming cardboard boxes into magical flying machines. Some of the most meaningful learning happens when time and space allow ideas to unfold naturally.

10 **Be their biggest cheerleader:** Children thrive when they feel seen, heard and celebrated. Make sure that every piece of artwork, every improvised dance move, every whispered song is acknowledged and valued. Ask about their work, listen to their ideas and show them that their creativity is important. A simple 'Tell me about your painting' instead of 'What is it?' makes all the difference.

Giving children the confidence to express themselves in whatever way feels right for them leads to joy and the unshakable belief that their creativity has immense value. In an educational world where creativity is too often treated as a luxury, nurturing it from the very beginning sends a powerful message – that the creative arts are not an extra, but an essential part of learning, thinking and being.

6.3
Planning Your Pedagogy

This chapter is about the educator's role in action; how you bring learning to life in everything you do. Whether it's leading a focused carpet session, working with a small group at a table or guiding children through play, it's the way we teach that makes all the difference. In this section, I'll share practical strategies that have been successful for me over the years. Fundamentally, it's about knowing when to lead, when to guide and when to step back and watch the magic unfold.

The EYFS Framework provides the foundation for teaching but leaves the approach up to us. It does not prescribe a particular teaching method, allowing educators to tailor their practice to suit the needs of their children and their context. This flexibility means that the way we deliver teaching, through carpet sessions, provision and play, becomes a crucial element of how we bring the framework to life.

Carpet Sessions: Building Focus and Foundations

Carpet time really is like stepping onto a stage. Your senses are heightened, your energy is focused, and you're primed for whatever comes your way (well, almost!).

It's a moment of magic, where you hold their attention, captivate their imaginations, sow seeds of intrigue and entice them in. With the right balance of structure, engagement and a sprinkle of theatre, you can turn those 10–15 minutes into something truly powerful. For me, carpet time is one of the most rewarding moments of the day.

It's also where we come together as a team – children and adults together, building relationships, sharing moments, and creating a classroom culture where learning is truly lived. I love seeing their faces light up as they make connections and become wide-eyed with wonder at something new. In these treasured moments, learning feels like an adventure. However, children should not be glued to the carpet for endless hours. Sessions need to be purposeful, well-paced, and appropriate to their developmental needs and are most effective when they are short and interactive.

So, how do we make every carpet session count? How do we ensure engagement from every child? Here are some tried-and-tested tips to spark curiosity and create moments that truly matter.

Practical Tips 6.3.1

Making Carpet Time Engaging and Impactful

- **Use visuals:** A picture, a diagram, a snippet from a video: a simple visual prompt can spark discussion and make abstract ideas tangible.
- **Bring in props:** A mysterious object in a box, a puppet or a special item from nature – anything that adds an element of intrigue!
- **Hidden surprises:** A reveal moment creates excitement. What's inside the bag today? Who will open the envelope?
- **Guest speakers:** Whether it's a real visitor, a recorded message or even a puppet in role, bringing in different 'voices' adds variety and engagement.
- **VIP moments:** Give a child a special role, helper, storyteller or question-master, to boost confidence and encourage leadership.
- **Music and songs:** A transition song, a rhythm to reinforce learning or a melody to set the mood. They all add an extra layer of fun.
- **Familiarity and routine:** A consistent structure builds security, while a little variety keeps them on their toes!
- **Praise and reward:** Celebrate effort, participation and those lightbulb moments with genuine awe and enthusiasm. Foster a sense of belonging by encouraging all children to participate, whether it's joining in with a shared chant, offering their thoughts during a story pause, or responding with agreed gestures during songs and rhymes.
- **Build anticipation:** Let them know something exciting is coming next, whether it's an activity, a challenge or a discovery waiting to be explored.
- **Involve your team:** Co-teaching moments, role-play scenarios or team-led storytelling can make sessions even richer.
- **Use video and technology:** A short clip, an animation or a sound effect can add an extra dimension to your session. For example, you might play a rocket countdown to launch your session into space, or use rainforest sounds to set off on a thrilling story adventure.
- **Encourage teamwork:** Think-pair-share, small group discussions or collective problem-solving, help them learn from each other as well as from you.
- **Flexibility:** Be responsive. If the children are restless or losing focus, adapt. Sometimes a quick movement break or a change in approach can recapture their attention.
- **Planning the session:** Keep it focused with a clear objective. Ask yourself: what golden nuggets of knowledge do I want them to walk away with? Whether it's understanding the properties of a triangle or absorbing the sequence of a familiar story, let that be your anchor, returning to it often so learning sticks.

Carpet time is all about connection and creating an atmosphere where learning feels alive. When done well, those moments on the carpet become the springboard for the rest of the day, setting children up with high expectations, ready to explore their environment with purpose.

Small Group Sessions: Personalised Learning in Action

Working with a small group provides an incredible opportunity to tailor teaching to children's specific needs, interests and abilities. These sessions allow for deeper interactions and moments of real connection. They should be focused, flexible and fun. I believe that children should come to you and not vice versa. Pulling children away from play can restrict their motivation.

- **Personalised and targeted:** Small group time is your chance to address the needs of individual children, whether it's reinforcing a tricky concept, introducing something new or stretching their thinking. Group size matters! Keep it small enough to give everyone your attention.
- **Interactive and engaging:** Keep activities hands-on and engaging. Use practical resources like manipulatives, story props or games to make the session come alive. For example, counting with small objects or acting out a story keeps learning tangible and fun.
- **Flexibility in focus:** Be ready to adjust based on the group's energy and responses. If something isn't clicking, try a different approach or simplify the task. Let children guide the session when their curiosity takes the lead. And remember – it doesn't have to be at a table.
- **Encourage collaboration:** Use group work to build social skills. Encourage turn-taking, sharing ideas and problem-solving together. It's amazing to see the dynamics of a group unfold as children work towards a shared goal or help each other overcome challenges.
- **Observation and feedback:** Small group time is the perfect setting to observe children closely. Take note of their progress, struggles and interests and use these insights to inform future planning. Celebrate their successes, no matter how small – they'll leave the session feeling accomplished.
- **Balance challenge and support:** Provide just enough support to keep children on track, but let them grapple with challenges, too. It's in these moments of struggle and perseverance that real growth happens.

Small group sessions are where learning becomes deeply personal. They give children the space to explore ideas and connect with you and their peers on a more individual level. These moments can be some of the most rewarding in your day.

Balancing Delivery Approaches

Effective teaching in the Early Years combines direct instruction, structured provision and open-ended play. The key is balance:

- **From teacher-led to child-led:** Carpet sessions and planned activities provide the foundations for learning, while provision and play allow children to deepen their understanding independently.
- **Adapting to children's needs:** Every class is unique. Some children may thrive with more structure, while others benefit from extended periods of free exploration. Responsive teaching ensures all children are supported.
- **Building relationships:** Above all, the teacher's presence makes the difference. The way we engage with children during carpet sessions, provision and play shapes how they see themselves as learners.

By blending these teaching elements, we create an environment where children can prosper: a place where they feel safe to explore, supported to try and inspired to achieve. This balance ensures that the EYFS Framework is not only adhered to but brought to life in a way that is dynamic and uniquely suited to every cohort.

Assessment

Assessment in the Early Years is a living, breathing process, woven into the fabric of daily interactions. It is the stage itself – ever-shifting, always alive – where each child's story unfolds with its own tempo, helping us see clearly where they are now, and where they're ready to go next. Progress flows in many directions, shaped by new experiences and deepened by reflection. It's messy and never linear. Small pockets of growth can appear unexpectedly and each small step forward lays a stronger foundation for what's to come.

Assessment follows no single path and obeys no fixed formula. What matters is knowing where a child began, recognising where they are now, and guiding them towards the next steps with care and intention. Conversations with colleagues reveal a broader picture, allowing for joined-up thinking that ensures every child's journey is understood in full.

Children develop at their own rate. Some surge forward, while others pause to strengthen foundations before moving ahead. Growth may be slow and steady, but it must never stall. Rushing ahead without securing the basics can be detrimental – each step must be rooted, each layer of learning firm before the next is added.

Assessment weaves itself through every moment: in playful exploration, in shared stories on the carpet, in the quiet concentration of a chosen task. Observing children in their natural domains, joining them in their world, and offering opportunities to master and revisit skills provides a true picture of progress.

Formative assessment happens constantly – an ongoing awareness of what a child knows, understands and can do at any one moment. These insights shape your teaching, ensuring learning remains responsive. Summative assessment, written at key points in the year, is a simple gathering of these insights, a professional reflection on the child's development over time. Assessment need not be time-consuming, nor should it pull focus away from what truly matters – being present with the children.

Every child follows their own unique pathway, progressing at their own momentum. Their interests, strengths, and experiences must be at the heart of their learning. An inclusive curriculum, alongside adaptive teaching and well-placed support, ensures every child moves forward from their own unique starting point.

Assessment is the quiet stagehand, adjusting the lights and setting the scene so every child can shine in their own time, with their own script, in a story still unfolding.

Six Practical and Powerful Assessment Tips for Early Years Teachers

1. **See the whole picture – talk, observe, reflect:** Assessment thrives in conversation. Talk to colleagues, share insights and build a complete picture of each child's progress. Observations in play, group activities and independent moments reveal what children truly know and can do. Step back, watch and reflect – learning unfolds in the in-between moments.

    How to do this:
    - Have regular informal check-ins with staff to discuss key observations.
    - Use professional dialogue during staff meetings to build a shared understanding of progress.
    - Consider using a 'snapshot board' where team members can jot down quick observations for discussion.

2. **Assessment happens in the everyday:** There's no need to stop learning to assess – assessment is embedded in every interaction. Carpet sessions, playtime, outdoor learning and snack-time chatter all offer rich opportunities to gather insights. Listen carefully, ask open-ended questions and capture learning as it happens.

    How to do this:
    - Keep a small notebook or use a voice recording app to note key learning moments.
    - Use mealtime conversations to assess language, turn-taking and social skills.
    - Observe how concepts introduced in teaching are reimagined in play, reshaped by children's curiosity and wonder.

3. **Focus on strengths and next steps:** Every child has a unique journey. Instead of searching for gaps, focus on strengths and build from them. Identify what they can do and consider the next small, achievable step. Growth is steady, and strong foundations are key – scaffold learning with care.

(Continued)

How to do this:

- Use 'I can see you are really confident with…' to highlight strengths before introducing a new challenge.
- Plan for small, manageable next steps instead of overwhelming leaps.
- Provide opportunities for children to revisit and embed learning through repeated experiences.

4. **Use play as your assessment tool:** Play is where children reveal their understanding most naturally. Step into their world, join their play and use careful questioning to assess knowledge and thinking. Set up familiar activities with slight variations to see if children can apply their skills in different contexts.

   How to do this:

   - Introduce a 'mystery challenge' in play areas to see how children apply their learning.
   - Rotate materials in role-play and small-world areas to observe how children adapt and respond.
   - Use playful questioning: 'What would happen if…?' or 'Can you show me another way to do that?'

5. **Keep it manageable – less paper, more purpose:** Excessive documentation takes time away from meaningful interactions. Use quick notes, voice recordings, or simple Post-its to capture learning on the go. Focus on quality over quantity. You are the professional at the heart of the classroom – keep assessments purposeful, sustainable, and rooted in what you know about each child.

   How to do this:

   - Use 'sticky note assessments' – brief, handwritten observations stuck in a shared space for later discussion.
   - Take photos or videos (with consent) as evidence rather than writing lengthy descriptions.
   - Keep assessment simple: Who? What? So what? – a child's name, the observation and what it tells you.

6. **Celebrate progress, however it comes:** Progress is not always linear, and every small step counts. A child mastering a skill they once found tricky, using new vocabulary or showing confidence in a familiar task are all milestones worth noting. Recognising these moments boosts motivation and helps children see themselves as capable learners.

   How to do this:

   - Create a 'Wow Wall' to showcase small but significant achievements.
   - Share progress with parents informally. Brief chats at pick-up time or postcards home help build a shared understanding.
   - Let children reflect on their own progress: 'What can you do now that you couldn't do before?'

By weaving assessment seamlessly into daily practice, teachers can nurture a rich and responsive learning environment. One where every child's journey is understood and thoughtfully guided.

Timely Interventions

Children are naturally inquisitive, often passionately leading their own learning journeys through free exploration and play. However, there are moments when they may hit a brick wall or need a gentle nudge to delve deeper into a concept. Thoughtful intervention is providing just the right amount of timely support and guidance to encourage children to overcome challenges and continue their learning in a progressive way. Thoughtful intervention refers to the intentional and measured involvement of an educator in a child's learning process. It's about knowing the exact moment to subtly step in to support and extend their learning and equally, when to take a step back and allow the child to explore independently. If you step in too soon, new discoveries are lost. Over-intervention can sometimes lead to an over-dependency on adult guidance and can diminish the child's ability to learn through trial and error.

Reasons Why you Might Step in

- **Stagnation:** When a child appears to be stuck or is repeating the same actions without progress, a gentle nudge can help them move forward.
- **Frustration:** If a child is showing signs of frustration or distress, an intervention can provide the support they need to overcome a challenge.
- **Lost interest:** If a child's engagement wanes, reintroducing an element of challenge or a new resource can rekindle their curiosity.

Therefore, one of the most impactful skills a practitioner can develop is the ability to intervene in a child's learning in a way that supports and extends their discovery, without diminishing their intrinsic motivation. This delicate balance between guiding and promoting autonomy is crucial. Let's explore now what makes an intervention 'thoughtful,' how to recognise when intervention is necessary and how to avoid common pitfalls that can disrupt a child's natural learning process.

- **Eye contact:** When engaging with a child, keep their eye contact and use encouraging gestures like smiles and nods to show your active involvement.
- **Honour their focus:** If a child is deeply engaged in an activity in provision, give them the space to continue without interruption. Support their concentration by stepping back when needed.
- **Enhance their language:** Introduce more ambitious vocabulary related to what the child is doing or saying to help extend their language skills.
- **Stay attuned:** Be fully present and attentive to the child's emotions, body language and actions. Keep your focus on the child rather than getting lost in your own thoughts.

- **Pose genuine questions:** Avoid asking questions with obvious answers. Show true curiosity to encourage deeper thinking and responses.
- **Keep an open perspective:** Avoid making assumptions about what the child is thinking or feeling. This allows you to ask more meaningful and open-ended questions.
- **Contribute your thoughts:** Make the conversation dynamic by sharing your own experiences or opinions but be sure to let the child lead the direction of the discussion.

In Summary: Directing the Journey – Planning, Performing and Reflecting

Throughout this chapter, we have explored the powerful connections that link planning, performing and reflecting and how these coincide across the Reception year. Like a motivated director guiding a theatre production, you and your Early Years team set the stage, crafting an environment where every child steps into the spotlight at their own pace, ready to shine in their own unique way. The Early Years Framework provides us with a script – the foundation, if you like – but the magic lies in how you bring it to life. The improvisation, the subtle cues, knowing when to pause and when to propel the story forward. I love this quote from John Spencer: 'Asking teachers to follow scripted curriculums is like asking artists to paint by numbers' (Spencer 2020). This sentiment highlights the risk of reducing teaching to a rigid formula. But true educators don't simply deliver lessons – they craft experiences. YOU carefully create the conditions where curiosity takes flight, where learning is immersive and deeply connected to the world beyond the classroom walls.

Within this grand performance, the interplay between teaching, play and observation is crucial. We step forward when needed, introducing new ideas and skills, yet we also know when to retreat, enabling children to take ownership of their learning – to experiment, to falter, to rise. Assessment is woven seamlessly into each and every day. It is in the quiet noticing and the way we carefully tune into children's play, acknowledging their moments of struggle and triumph. It does not disrupt learning – it enriches it, allowing us to see beyond the surface, to understand the depths of a child's thinking and illuminate their next steps with clarity. It is found in the way a child explains their thinking, in the problem they solve without realising it, in the joy of a new skill mastered. Thoughtful interventions become the gentle whispers from backstage, just enough to encourage but never to overshadow. Learning is not a linear path but an intricate, looping, iterative performance, rehearsed and refined through daily experiences. This chapter celebrates the craft of teaching as an art form; an intuitive, responsive and profoundly human endeavour, where we do not simply follow a prescribed script, but breathe life into it, ensuring that every child leaves the stage feeling seen, heard and ready for their next act.

References

Department for Education (DfE) (2023) *Development Matters: Non-statutory Curriculum Guidance for the Early Years Foundation Stage*. Available at: www.gov.uk/government/publications/development-matters--2/development-matters

Department for Education (DfE) (2025) *Early Years Foundation Stage Statutory Framework: For Group and School-based Providers*. (effective 1 September 2025). London: Department for Education.

National Literacy Trust (n.d.) *What is Literacy?* Available at: https://literacytrust.org.uk/information/what-is-literacy/

Spencer, J. (2020) *Empowered Teachers Empower Students*. Available at: https://spencereducation.com/empowered-teachers-empower-students/

7
Final Curtain Call

Inspiring Early Years Educators Everywhere

So here we are, at the final chapter of this journey. Throughout this book, we've delved into the depths of Early Years education, exploring its joys, challenges and transformative power. Now, as the spotlight fades on my current reflections within these pages, I am reminded of the vital role that current and future Early Years educators play in shaping the lives of young learners around the globe.

Each day, educators hold the power to change a child's path. My dream as a collective from hereon in is simple: for us all to continue to champion Early Years teachers worldwide in their noble pursuit of nurturing young minds and hearts. As we reflect on the pages we've turned and the anecdotes and advice that I've shared, I am reminded of the infinite potential that resides within each child and the pivotal role that united educators play in unlocking it. Together, we have explored the wonders of Early Years education, celebrating its magic and embracing its challenges with courage and resilience.

As I look back on my rich and rewarding journey in education, I am immensely grateful and proud of the countless moments that have shaped my path; the laughter, the lightbulb moments, the key milestones and the lessons learned through both triumphs and tribulations. My EYFS journey began back in 2015, after a fulfilling career as a KS1 and KS2 teacher since qualifying in 2000. Don't get me wrong, I absolutely loved teaching KS2. I cherished the camaraderie we built, the thought-provoking questions they asked, the depth of enquiry, the shared humour and the moments of joy that filled our school days. Yet, stepping into EYFS felt like coming home. Each day was filled with awe and wonder, and the magic of that first year in Reception was like nothing I'd experienced before. The Reception year is sacred. The children akin to sponges, soaking up every single experience you offer them with genuine enthusiasm and endless curiosity. Me as their proud and happy guide, their companion and unwavering supporter. The astronomical progress that children make in that one crucial year, academically, socially and emotionally, is nothing short of extraordinary and being part of that transformation is a privilege I hold extremely close to my heart.

Looking back, my career has been shaped by moments that remain etched in my heart; moments of joy, moments of challenge and moments that transformed me as an educator. I still remember walking into my very first classroom. It was a space brimming with possibility but also tinged with overwhelming uncertainty. I had so much to learn but I threw myself into every moment. Those small victories; the first 'I did it!', the first parents evening, the first time I saw a child's eyes light up with understanding – all of these carried me forward, step by meaningful step.

Seeing children grow in confidence, master new skills and find their voices is what makes this job so rewarding. They are the force that drives us, day after day. The children are never the challenge; they're the reason. We follow their lead.

The real challenge? Finding your people. The right culture, a leadership team that truly values Early Years and a network of supportive parents who stand beside you. Those are the elements that can make or break your experience. And when those pieces are missing, the role can become overwhelming. These struggles don't stem from the children but from the broader system. A system that sometimes feels out of step with the magic and importance of Early Years education. A system that doesn't always see us.

Far more than simply an 'introduction to education', these pivotal years play a defining role in a child's growth and personal identity. Every major milestone achieved, each newfound strength developed and every moment of true connection sets the stage for everything that follows. The learning that happens in Early Years is not a matter of ticking phonics boxes or nudging children towards school readiness in a linear, one-size-fits-all way. It is far deeper, richer and more foundational.

Over the last 25 years, my many rewarding roles have led me to countless Early Years settings, where learning is at the heart of every moment. I am regularly in a state of awe at the dedication and expertise of Early Years staff, whose unwavering commitment ensures children receive the highest quality care and education. Yet they do so while facing countless daily challenges including stretched resources, increasing expectations and the ongoing necessity to advocate for the importance of Early Years education. If we are serious about giving children the best possible start in life, then we must be serious about giving those who teach them the respect, resources and development they deserve.

But despite it all, Early Years educators everywhere persevere. Because you know what you do matters. You know that every connection you build and every child you champion is a step towards a brighter future. That is the power of this work and that is why you keep going.

I vividly recall the moment our team was awarded EYFS Ofsted Outstanding. While it wasn't the ultimate reward (that came from our internal successes and intrinsic motivation), it was a validation that meant so much. To be recognised for our hard work and dedication felt like proof that we were on the right track. And let me tell you, I didn't shy away during the Ofsted process. I stood my ground, asked as many questions as I answered, and demonstrated my unwavering commitment to knowing each child as an individual – not through paperwork, but through presence, care and daily connection.

Remember, EYFS is not a one-size-fits-all framework. What works brilliantly in one setting may not suit another. Trust your instincts as a professional. Only you truly know your children, your cohort, your setting and your community. Fleeting visitors don't live and breathe your environment the way you do. They aren't there in the everyday moments, the challenges and the victories. You and your team are immersed in your setting every day, and that gives you the authority and autonomy (in my opinion) to make the decisions that are right for your children and community. Trust your gut. Bring your team along with you. Build a culture of collaboration and continuous improvement. And, above all, never let anyone dull your 'Early Years sparkle'. Believe me, over the years, plenty of people have tried to dull mine. But here I am, still standing, still smiling and still deeply proud of what I've achieved. As an EYFS teacher, I know I've made a difference. And as a leader, I know how to value the people around me, to create a motivated and united team and to build something truly special together. That's a legacy I'll always hold close.

I am truly at my happiest when I am in a Reception class. Those years were the absolute highlight of my career. I can't help but smile when I think of the difference I made to the children in my care, knowing the foundation we built together would carry them forward.

When you're in the right school, surrounded by supportive colleagues and working within a culture that uplifts and truly values you, being a Reception teacher truly is the best job in the world.

To close, education should stir something deep within. It should challenge, encourage and stretch every mind towards something greater. Education should always offer more than answers; it should awaken relentless curiosity. The world does not need echoes; it needs thinkers, dreamers, doers...

A true education does not seek to shape children to fit a mould. It meets them with patience and purpose; where they are, as they are. It nurtures their spirit, equips their mind and gently opens doors. It does not dictate the path but clears the way, so they might walk it with greater confidence, curiosity and courage. And when they step forward, centre stage, steady in the spotlight, heads high, eyes sharp, ideas bold... we will know they are ready for the next act to begin.

Index

accessibility, enhanced, 26
acetylcholine, 63
action research, 12–14
active engagement, 64
active listening, 48–51, 56
Adoniou, M., 25, 38
anticipation building, 104
arts and craft area, 35–36
asking questions, 47, 49, 110
assessment, 106–109
assumptions, avoiding, 110
attention, 50
audio recording, 13

balanced classroom, 24–27
balancing delivery approaches, 106
Barrett, P., 25
barrier games, 51–52
bilingual learners, 57, 59
The Black Nursery Manager, 27
blueprints, 32, 37, 82
books
 baskets, 30
 and literacy, 94
 sparking joy, 30
 treasure chests, 31
 under-table nooks, 31
Bottrill, G., 38
Britton, J., 45
Bryce-Clegg, A., 39

caddies, 37
caregivers. *See* parents/caregivers
carpet time, 103–105
Characteristics of Effective Teaching and Learning, 81
Children's Play Council and Playlink, 62
circle time, 17, 58
 for connection, 18
 conversations, 49
 storytelling, 51
classroom
 balanced, 24–27
 colour in, 25–27
 culturally responsive, 56
 displays, 37–38
 indoor, 28

layout and learning zones, 29
organisation for maximum learning, 27–28
well-defined learning areas, 28
clipboards, 37
Coe, J., 25
collaboration, 11–12, 61
 dialogue and, 80
 joy and, 79
 small group time, 105
 teamwork and, 32
collaborative play, 31–32
collaborative problem-solving, 82
colour, in classroom, 25–27
communication, 91, 92–93
 building through play and interaction, 54–55
 closing gap, 55–56
 effective, 10–11
 encouraging, 46–49
 inclusive of forms, 53
 non-verbal, 57–58
 one-way, 53
 respectful, 12
 supporting through interaction, 53–55
 See also language
community engagement, 15–16
concentration, 50
confident communicators, 58
confident speaking, 46–49
conflict resolution, 17–18, 20, 88
construction area, 31–32
continuous provision, 13, 65–67
co-opted play, 63–64
creativity, 35–36, 100–102
critical thinking, 64–65
cultural capital, 10, 45, 55, 59, 99, 101
culturally responsive classroom, 56
curiosity, 30, 65, 69, 77, 79
curriculum
 assessment and impact, 84–85
 building, 94
 creating, 82–85
 designing, 73, 75
 in EYFS Framework, 83
 knowing about children, 83–84
 meaningful learning experiences, 84

play-based, awe-inspiring, 79
progression and learning intentions, 84
review, reflect and adapt, 85
vision and values, 83

descriptive comments, 47
descriptive talk, 52
dialogue
  missing opportunities for, 53
  opportunities for, 52
  reading, 48
disadvantaged children, 10, 45, 55–56
displays, inspirational, 35, 36
dopamine, 63
drama, 49, 100

Early Learning Goals (ELGs), 83
echo games, 51
Education Endowment Foundation (EEF), 47–48
effective communication, 10–11
effective continuous provision, 66–67
emotional responses, 89
empathy, 61, 93
enabling environments, 79–80
endorphins, 63
enthusiasm, 11, 16, 79, 95, 100, 113
envelopes, 37–38
environmental connects, 70–71
environments
  enabling, 79–80
  intentional, adaptable, 77
  inviting and provoking, 66
  well-organised and inviting, 81
  See also classroom
expression
  confident, 81–82
  love for, 37–38
  self-expression, 35, 93
  vibrant and inclusive art area to ignite, 35–36
Expressive Arts and Design, 100–101
eye contact, 109
EYFS Framework, 73, 75, 106, 113–115
  anti-discriminatory practice, 76
  enabling environments, 79–80
  equality of opportunity, 76
  foundation for teaching, 103
  home corner and role-play area in, 32–33
  learning and development, 80–82
  outdoor learning, 39
  overarching principles, 76–82
  partnerships with families, 76
  positive relationships in action, 78–79
  quality and consistency, 76
  reshaping, 16
  revised, 2
  secure foundation, 76
  supporting children's literacy development, 93
  unique child, 76–78
EYFS Ofsted Outstanding, 2–3, 114

feedback
  from peers, parents and children, 13
  small group time, 105
flexibility, 97, 103–105
focus
  building, 103
  honour, 109
formative assessment, 106–107
free play, 62–63
free resources, 68
frustration, 109

gamma-aminobutyric acid (GABA), 63
gardening projects, 40
gender, 34
goals sharing, 7–8
Grenier, J., 1
gross motor play, 90

harmonious team building, 5–7
HEAD project, 25
high-quality conversations, 56
home corner, 32–33

imaginative play, 33, 34, 53–55
imaginative role-playing, 61, 63
innovation, 100–102
inspirational displays, 35, 36
interaction
  communication and, 53–55
  meaningful, 80
  one-to-one, 55–56
  positive, 18
  practitioner with children, 78, 80
  small group, 105
IPA England, 62

Kinderly, 57
kindness, 11–12, 17–18, 62, 78–79, 89

language, 91, 94
  clear, 47
  descriptive talk, 52
  development, 33, 47–48
  enhancing, 109
  frequent conversations, 52
  interactive storytelling, 52
  language-poor environment, 53
  language-rich environment, 52–53
  model expressive, 54–55
  modelling, 52

in play, 53–55
  power of, 45–46, 92–93
  promoting speaking skills to boost, 48–49
  rich play areas, 49
  role in emotional development, 88–89
large-scale art, 40
learning and development, 80–82
learning space, 24–27
left-handed learners, 90
limited vocabulary, 53
lined paper, 37–38
listening games, 50–51
literacy, 93–95
loss of interest, 109

mathematics, 95–97
meaningful interactions, 80
meaningful learning, 84
meaningful relationships, 78
mini displays, 31
mistakes, celebrating, 48
multilingual learners, 57, 59
music-based movement, 91, 101, 104

National Literacy Trust, 93
National Playing Fields Association (NPFA), 62
natural curiosity, 30
natural elements, 26, 30
natural light, 30
nature, power of, 68
non-verbal communication, 57–58, 59
Nuffield Early Language Intervention (NELI), 56
nursery rhymes, 49, 51

observation, small group time, 105
one-to-one interactions, 55–56
one-way communication, 53
open dialogue, 20, 48
open-ended questions, 48, 54, 56, 64–65, 92
opinion corners, 49
oracy, 46, 48, 56, 59
outdoor learning, 39–40
outdoor play, 39, 67–69
outdoor space, physical development, 90
over-intervention, 109
over-reliance, 53
overstimulation, avoiding, 26
overuse of screens/passive activities, 53
oxytocin, 63

parents/caregivers
  active engagement, 80
  in child's language development, 55
  feedback from, 13
  involvement, encouraging, 59
  in supporting educational performance, 14–15
partner listening, 51–52
Peacock, A., 46
peers
  feedback from, 13
  meaningful relationships with, 78
  peer-to-peer relationships, 17
Pemberton, L., 27
personalised learning, 105
Personal, Social and Emotional Development (PSED), 87–89
personal touches, 24, 26, 27
phonics, 93, 114
physical confidence, 89
physical development, 68, 89–91
planning
  blueprints and, 32
  classroom layout and learning zones, 29
  involving children in, 34
  for learning and development, 76
  pedagogy, 103–110
  for physical development, 89, 91
  session, 104
play, 61–62
  as assessment tool, 108
  autonomy in, 64–65
  as celebration of diversity, 71
  collaborative, 31–32
  continuous provision, 65–67
  co-opted, practical strategies for, 63–64
  as driver of intrinsic motivation, 65
  as emotional exploration, 63
  environments, 63–64
  executive function and, 62
  free, 62–63
  gross motor, 90
  imaginative, 33, 34, 53–55
  integrating joy into, 64
  language in, 53–55
  language-rich play areas, 49
  learning and growth, 69–70
  literacy through, 94–95
  materials, easy access to, 68
  opportunities, 18
  outdoor, 39, 67–69
  promoting, 64–65
  reflection role in, 71
  resilience building, 62
  transformative power, 70–71
  uninterrupted playtimes, 65
  water, 40
  writing in, 94
positive interactions, 18
positive relationships, 78

post-it notes, 37–38
practitioners, 109
　dialogue and collaboration, 80
　encouraging and supportive language, 79, 82
　interactions with children, 78, 80
　responsive, 77
　supporting and extending learning, 77
printing, 53
problem-solving, 54, 61, 64, 82, 97

questioning, 48, 71, 96

reading
　aloud, 48–49
　area, 29–30, 81
　dens, 31
　dialogic, 48
　nooks, 30–31
　oasis, creating, 30–31
　themed corners, 31
real-life inspirations, 32
refining, power of, 67
reflection journals, 13
reflective educators, 13–14
reflective practices, 12–14
relationships
　building, 16, 106
　meaningful, 78
　peer-to-peer, 17
　positive relationships, 78
　trusting, 88
resilience, 39, 61, 66, 69, 113
　building, 23, 62, 70
　emotional, 39, 62
resources
　for continuous provision, 66
　free, 68
　incorporating, 26
　open-ended, 35
revisiting, power of, 67
reward, 2–3, 80, 103–105, 113, 114
rhythm games, 51, 78, 91
risk-taking, 66
　encouraging, 90
　outdoor play and, 70
　secure environment for, 88
role-playing, 17, 25, 42, 65, 100
　additional setup, 33–34
　creating areas, 54
　and drama, 49
　in home corner, 77, 80
　imaginative, 61, 63
　inclusive and engaging, 34
　opportunities for, 59
　and storytelling, 28, 31

rote instruction, 53
Rowling, J. K., 46

scaffolding, 13, 88, 91
scientific thinking, 98, 99
self-care, 89
self-confidence, 61
self-determination, 89
self-expression, 35, 93
self-regulation, 66, 88
sense of belonging and inclusion, 78–79
sensory experiences, 38–39
sensory exploration, 40
serotonin, 63
shared goals, 7–8
shared responsibility, 12
shared vision, 7–10
'Show and Tel' sessions, 51
small-group interactions, 55–56
small group time, 105
social learning theory, 48
social play, 64
soft lighting, 34
songs, 49, 104
sound, 34, 104
　matching games, 51
　scavenger hunt, 51
　See also voice
spatial reasoning, 62–63, 96
speaking
　confident, 46–49
　promoting skills, 48–49
special educational needs and disabilities (SEND), 81
stagnation, 109
STEP approach, 48
stories, 30–31
storytelling, 49, 56, 92
　circle time, 51
　encouraging, 55
　interactive, 30, 52
　past to life through, 98–99
storytime, 48–49, 52
success
　celebrating, 95
　steps lead to, 97
summative assessment, 106

Talk Boost, 56
targeted, small group time, 105
team building, 5–7
teamwork, 6, 18, 32, 104
thoughtful intervention, 109
timely interventions, 109–110
transformative power, 1, 61, 70–71, 113
Treasure of Triumphs jar, 18
trust

building, 11–12, 78
culture, 9
relationships, 88
turn-taking, 17, 49, 56, 88–89, 105
TV broadcaster, 52

Understanding the World to life, 97–100
uninterrupted play, 63, 65
unique children, understanding, 76–78

video recording, 13, 32, 104
vision, 7–8
　shared, 7–10
　and values, 83
visuals, 30, 35, 104
　aids, 11, 52, 56
　clutter, 26
　displays, 80
　extension of learning, 37
　flow, 26
　markers, 26
　noise, 26, 42
　story inspirations, 30
　timetables, 81

vocabulary
　activities, 49
　limited, 53
　new, 47, 53
voice
　finding, 46–49
　sharing and connecting, 79
　with wonder and curiosity, 77, 80
Voice 21 Oracy Framework, 7–8, 46, 56
Voltaire, 36
Vygotsky, L.S., 48

water play, 40
Whitebread, D., 63–64
Wright, S., 38
writing
　areas, 36
　belts, 37
　frames, 37
　incorporating, 37
　passion for, 37–38
　play in, 94
　reasons to, 38
　tools, 37

www.ingramcontent.com/pod-product-compliance
Lightning Source LLC
Chambersburg PA
CBHW051352070526
44584CB00025B/3736